Soraya believes:
You are magical.
You are mystical.
You are spiritual.

Soraya is a white witch, and an internationally renowned author and psychic. She is the resident psychic astrologer and psychic agony aunt for *My Weekly,* one of the UK's leading magazines.

Soraya is the author of *Tarot, Book of Spells, Enhance your Psychic Powers, Runes, The Kitchen Witch, The Witch's Companion, The Little Book of Spells, The Little Book of Cord and Candle Magick,* and, forthcoming, *The Practical Witch.*

Soraya is the founder of the Lightworkers Foundation Reiki Training Courses which were endorsed by the SQA.

You can contact Soraya via her website at
www.soraya.co.uk

BOOK
OF
SPELLS

SORAYA

Dedication

Thanks and blessings to my husband Martin and
my youngest daughter Tori whose patience, support
and assistance have been invaluable.

My life is mine that I can change
By the power of my will.
Yours you do with as you wish,
Or change and be fulfilled.

Published 2017 by Geddes & Grosset, an imprint of
The Gresham Publishing Company Ltd,
Academy Park, Building 4000, Gower Street,
Glasgow, G51 1PR, Scotland

First published 2001. Reprinted 2001, 2002, 2004, 2006,
2008 (twice), 2010, 2015, 2016 (twice), 2017

ISBN 978 1 84205 108 5

Printed and bound in the EU

Positive thoughts and actions can work miracles

Like most people today, I choose to believe that there is a higher power at work in all our lives.

In this book I will demonstrate that our own inner strength is vastly increased by having a clearer focus and understanding of how to connect with the higher power within us.

I will also explain the value of creating the right environment and the importance of drawing strength from the higher power.

This book contains 46 different spells using everyday items, candles, oils and symbols to help you empower your life for the better. For those who are interested in the healing aspect and the magical properties of flowers, I have included some interesting and simple remedies like my granddaughter's favourite, Magik Marigold Syrup.

I was born in 1947, in Bethlehem, on Christmas Day, to an Arabian mother and a Scottish father, and came to Scotland with my parents when I was just 3 months old. I was named after my Arabian grandmother and the name Soraya means 'the brightest star in the galaxy of seven stars'.

My life has been a series of coincidences and sometimes life-shattering events that have made me who I am today. Years of study, and my own life experiences, have shown me that individuals can create their own futures by using the power within themselves. I want to share this knowledge with you in this book.

Blessings

Contents

part one:
magik by the light of the moon

Preparing Your Magikal Tools 51

Why Cast a Circle? 59

part two:
making the magik happen

part one:

magik by the light of the moon

The Magik has Already Begun

Do you believe that there is a reason for everything? Do you believe that if you wish hard enough anything is possible? Do you believe that you can do more in your life? Have you noticed that sometimes what you want happens almost before you express the desire?

Where are you now? Standing in a shop or sitting in your favourite chair at home?

Perhaps someone has given you this book – perhaps you have been drawn to it – either way the magik has already begun.

But what is magik?

Magik is the art of causing change in accordance with your will. In other words, magik is the art of making things happen, as you would wish them to. Magik is simply the manipulation of energy.

Some people are afraid of magik, and so they should be because magik is powerful stuff. Some say that magik is black or evil, white or good, but the truth is there is no black, evil, good or white magik – it's all the same. There are, however, good people and evil people. If your heart is filled with evil or wicked intentions then this book is not for you.

But then again, perhaps it is because this book may have come to you so that you can change your ways. The first rule of magik is:

And it harm none so be it.

The reason for this is simple: whatever you put out will come back to you threefold. In other words, if you send out good wishes or words then three times that amount will come back to you. If you send out bad wishes or words then the same will apply: three times that amount will come back to you.

To understand this, you have to understand a little more of how magik works. When we desire something the thing we normally do is to think of it. Then we might talk about it to someone close. Some people take things a little further and do something about achieving what they want. If it is an item that can be purchased, they might start saving for it. Making the magik happen is as simple as that, but with knowledge and practice it can go much further.

Be careful what you wish for

When I was a child, I was always wishing for something. My mother would tell me to be careful about what I wished for because I might get it and then be sorry. It was years before I began to really understand what she meant. Any time that I questioned her she would tell me that I would understand when I was older.

One day, I asked for new ice skates and my mum said that I could not have them. I pleaded with her and finally she explained that she could not afford them. I replied that I wished we were very rich and could afford everything. My mum was furious. She turned to me, pointing her finger, shaking it at me in anger and told me never to wish for such a thing. I was shocked at her reaction. I only wanted to be rich, what was wrong with that? Mum explained to me that I would feel very bad if my wish came true as a result of something bad happening to someone. I still could not understand so she almost whispered her fears.

'What would you feel like if someone you loved very much died and left you a lot of money?'

That made me stop and think. She was right. I would have been heartbroken if I had lost someone I loved.

You might wish for a new car and think there is nothing wrong with that. But what sequence of events might have to happen to enable you to get your dream? The money you need for the car might come from an unfortunate source like the insurance money for an accident or injury. You might wish a passionate lover to come into your life and when he or she arrives, the person might be passionate and exciting but might not touch your heart with love. I can speak from experience on that one.

One day I spilled some coffee on my lovely new cream-coloured, canvas espadrilles. I decided to wash them to get rid of the stain. Later, after they had dried in the sun, I inspected them only to discover that there was no difference. The stain was still there. As I looked at them, I realised that the stain was in the shape of the sun. Not realising what I was doing, I began to create a magik spell. I took a coloured pen and drew round the stain. Now that I had done this on one shoe, I had to balance it up on the other one too. I drew a crescent moon on the other shoe. I tried both shoes on and admired my handiwork. I began to think of the symbols that I had used.

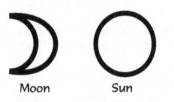

Moon   Sun

The sun is masculine and the moon is feminine ... mm! I did not have someone special in my life so I thought it would be fun to see if drawing a masculine symbol on my shoe brought someone into my life. I was beginning to get quite carried away with myself. My sign is Capricorn so I drew the appropriate glyph on the shoe with the moon symbol. Now I really had to think. What would be an exciting sign to be in a relationship with? Well, I knew that the sign of Scorpio was quite a sexy sign so without further ado I drew the glyph for Scorpio on the shoe with the sun symbol on it. I needed some action in my life so on went the symbol for Mars and, to balance this, the other shoe was given the symbol for Venus.

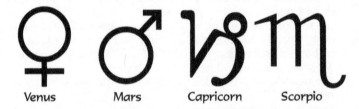

Venus   Mars   Capricorn   Scorpio

I was very happy with the finished result and was proud to wear my previously ruined shoes. If only I had realised! Within the week, someone who was born under the sign of Scorpio befriended me. He was passionate, sexy and attractive and although this certainly brought some action into my life, he did not love me, nor I him. The tragedy was though, that when I tried to tell him how I felt, he did not want to listen. No matter what I said or did, I was not able to convince him that this relationship was not what I wanted. I cried many tears over this and eventually I had to hurt his feelings and damage his pride. I felt bad and I am sure that he did too and, to this day, he has never forgiven me.

I created magik without thinking about what I was doing and without considering the effects that my magik would have on another person's life. And that brings us back to the first rule of magik:

And it harm none.

You may wonder in what way this inadvertent spell came back to me. Simple really – the next person that I dated broke my heart.

Never speak ill of anyone

The power of magik begins with the words that you speak and the depth of feeling behind these words. I always tell people I know, and particularly my students, to watch what they say and never to speak ill of anyone. Recently a student of mine called and asked me if it was possible to hex someone by accident. Hex means to wish ill on another person.

'What do you think you have done?' I asked.

At first, she was a little hesitant about telling me, perhaps doubting her own magikal skills.

'I had a conversation with my boyfriend before the Christmas holidays and he told me of a secretary who was causing problems in the office. I told him that she deserved to be fired and he told me that she never would because she had been with the company for a very long time.'

My student then went on to tell me that when her boyfriend went back to work, he found out that the secretary had been fired. They were both amazed by this piece of news but for very different reasons.

My student had indeed hexed this person.

'Perhaps it's just a coincidence,' she said, trying to ease her troubled conscience.

Perhaps it was, but was she willing to take the chance?

'What can I do to fix things, I don't want to feel guilty or have this hanging over my head?'

I told her to light a small candle and dedicate it to the secretary, to wish her success in her chosen field and to wish that she would find a new job that she would like as soon as possible.

The second rule of magik is, if you think that you have made a mess of something, do something to fix it immediately. If you utter negative words to or about someone, immediately say:

I take these words back and wish you well.

Powerful stuff this magik!

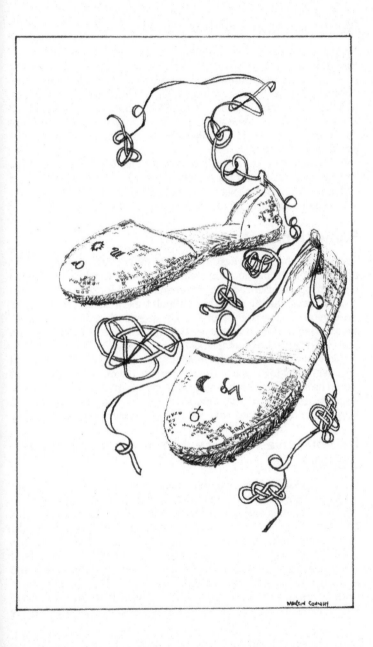

Never interfere with a person's will

Never, ever, interfere with another person's will. You may think at this point that you only want to create magik for yourself but what if you were in a situation where your best friend had separated from his or her partner or lover. You might be tempted then to magik them together again. This is probably the worst thing that you could do! If they are destined to be together, then they will be and if they are destined to be apart then they should be left to get on with the painful experience of parting.

You know what they say: 'That which does not kill us makes us stronger and wiser.' Richard Bach in his book *Illusions* puts it in a rather more interesting way when he says: 'Here is a test to find out if your mission on earth is complete. If you are alive it is not.'

Some things are meant to be

Experiences that we are destined to have, for whatever reason, should not be changed. That does not mean that you cannot do something to help during experiences. You can create a spell for someone to have peace of mind during his or her difficult time. You can create a spell to help someone recover his or her self-esteem, which is so often damaged during the break-up of a relationship. You can also create a spell that will draw in love and friendship.

I will repeat that: you can create a spell that will draw in love and friendship. Not to draw a particular person towards you because that would be interfering with their will. If you do attempt this and create a spell to draw a particular person toward you then you may end up having that relationship but it would be a very unhappy one.

Do you have to be a witch or a wizard to cast a spell?

I have been asked that question so many times. The answer is simple. No, you do not have to be, but only a witch or a wizard can teach you the fundamentals and the ethics of spell casting. You can learn this craft by studying with a mentor or by reading some of the many books that are available. This question is usually asked when someone has the desire to cast a spell or make magik happen in his or her life. If you are asking that question, I suppose the real answer is that you probably are a witch or a wizard.

The word witch comes from the words wise or wisdom and originally witches were called the wise ones. Witches are healers who study natural remedies and the influences of the cycles of moon and the planets. Witches seek to harm none, knowing the energy they send out comes back threefold.

I discovered that I was a witch or a pagan when someone gave my sixteen-year-old daughter a book on witches. Panicking, I took the book from her and told her that I would read it first and if it was suitable then I would give it back to her. Within the first two chapters, I discovered that I was reading about things that I had believed most of my life and, to be truthful, I felt as though this book had been written about me. I could liken different experiences that I had had as a child and as an adult to those in this book.

I knew that the things that the authors talked of in the first few pages had been with me all my life. It was this same sense of knowing that had always made me feel different and had alienated me from others. This was the first time that I had heard the word Wicca and the first time that I had understood the word paganism.

What is paganism?

My understanding of paganism until that time had been people who do not believe in or worship God. In fact, The *Collins English Dictionary* describes a pagan as a person without any religion – a heathen.

Recently the subject of pagans came up in a group discussion and one woman stated that pagans worshipped Satan. This makes me feel quite sad.

I am a pagan. I do believe in God and I believe that I have a greater understanding of God than I ever had before. The word pagan was derived from the Latin word *pagus*, which means countryside. This then became *paganus*, which referred to someone who lived in the countryside. The word heathen originally meant heath dweller.

The three principles of the Pagan Federation, of which I am a member and former office bearer, are:

1 Love for and kinship with nature. Reverence for the life force and its ever-renewing cycles of life and death.
2 A positive morality in which each individual is responsible for the discovery and development of their true nature in harmony with the outer world and the community. This is often expressed as 'Do what you will as long as it harms none'.
3 Recognition of the Divine, which transcends gender, acknowledging both the male and female aspect of Deity.

A pagan is someone who believes in a supreme Being who is above, below and all around us. A being that is in the life-giving air that we breath, in the fire that warms us, in the water that washes us clean and sustains us and in the earth that carries our weight.

A pagan is someone who recognises that this supreme being is made up of masculine and feminine elements, as we all are. A god and goddess combined (see the illustration of this on page 24). Father God who reigns above us and Mother Earth beneath our feet.

Think of that for a moment and realise why pagans all over the world are saddened by the destruction of our Mother Earth.

It is these same pagans who meet on regular intervals at badly littered, overgrown and neglected ancient sites and spend their own precious time cleaning up the mess that is left by others.

A pagan is someone who respects the choices that each individual makes in practising their beliefs. Paganism is not a religion, paganism is a faith.

Pagans believe in observing the laws and signs of nature, believe in life after death, believe in the God-given gifts of healing and believe in the power of word, deed and action – magik.

If you have reached a stage in your life where you believe that there must be more, if you feel as though you are searching, as I did then perhaps this path is for you.

Is Wicca a new religion?

Wicca or paganism is not a religion at all. Wicca is a Goddess-based belief system that can be dated back at least 25,000 years. However, its usage as a term used for those who practice paganism is relatively new. Pagan faiths have existed on most continents since history began and there are many disciplines. Some people are drawn to the Egyptian philosophy, others to Druidism. Some are drawn to the Anglo Saxon tradition and others follow a Native American path. Some people are known as kitchen witches, green witches or solos. Green witches focus on the earth and are likely to be involved in replenishing or restocking wasteland to introduce trees, shrubs, flora and fauna that may be dying because of pollution or mankind's general neglect or abuse. They may also be involved in the production of natural herbal remedies. Kitchen witches, whilst being supportive of green issues will also produce their own self-grown herbal remedies and potions but on a much smaller scale. A solo can be a green witch or a kitchen witch. The term means that they work alone rather than in a group. They may, from time to time, join other groups for celebrations.

As with all faiths there are offshoots and varieties and that is

because everyone is different and their needs are different too. Wicca or paganism is something that you believe in and practise in a way that suits you.

Imagine a time long ago

The roots of paganism are buried deep in history. To understand this time, thousands of years ago, imagine a time when our ancestors lived in tribes or clans – no means of communication other than the spoken word, no means of transport other than one's own feet.

Life was harsh in those far off days and if you wanted to eat you had to find your food in your surroundings. Wild animals were hunted for meat and clothing and people would forage for edible plants. Before winter came, food and firewood had to be gathered and stored to last through this difficult season and the nights would be cold and dark if supplies ran out.

The children, the youths, the maidens, the hunters or warriors, the mothers and the old wise women or medicine women would be safe in the cave, gathered round a camp fire listening to the stories that the elders would tell.

The elders would speak of the things that they had learned from their elders when they were young. Sometimes perhaps they would sing their stories and everyone would join in and this would make these lessons, for that's what they were, easier to understand.

The elders would speak of the stars in the night sky, of the sun and the moon and how each morning the sun would chase away the moon but as the sun slept, the moon would reappear. Their knowledge of the stars and the planets in the night sky gave them the wisdom that helped them to survive in those bygone days. As the younger ones grew to maturity they would in turn teach others. The wise ones, having spent many years watching their clan grow and watching seasons change had a great understanding of time and the patterns of nature. These old men, once hunters or warriors themselves but too old to hunt now, had a valuable place in the society. To the warriors or hunters, they would tell stories of their grandfathers and of hunts of which they in turn had been told. Mostly these old men would be shamans.

Often someone who was disabled or disfigured in some way and could not hunt would be regarded as special and singled out to be the apprentice of a wise one. Perhaps they recognised that where one sense was weakened another sense was strengthened. At certain times the shaman would speak with the spirits and ask for guidance on matters concerning the clan. Many different methods were used to do this but old traditions were always adhered to.

The old women had their place in the scheme of things too. As they grew up they would have been taught by the wise woman or medicine woman of their time of the properties of the herbs and plants that they gathered. They would have amassed great knowledge and understanding of all the plants, the times that they grew, the best places to find them, and their medicinal properties. They would know through practised skills which plants would heal or treat certain conditions. Traditionally these skills would be passed from mother to her first-born daughter. If they had no daughter, they would watch as the youngsters grew and they would choose the girl who showed most promise to carry on this wisdom.

Soon the nights would grow shorter. Those who survived the harsh winter would venture out to the fields or plains to begin hunting for fresh meat and gathering again those wild plants and herbs. This would be a time of celebration. During this first celebration people could now look forward to the arrival of spring.

After the spring equinox the people of the clan would be aware of the longer days, the grass, green beneath their feet, and the skies above them, blue. Flowers would begin to bloom and new life would be everywhere. Hunting, fishing and farming or gathering could begin in earnest. Fresh food would be the staple diet but the harshness of the winter that had passed would not be forgotten so food would be dried and stored for future use.

As the Wheel of the Year turned and summer approached children played happily, lovers kissed and laughter filled the air. Traditionally this would be a time for members of many clans to make plans to meet each other. Food would be in good supply so some would be set aside for sharing with neighbouring clans. Romance would be in the air and young men and women would be thinking of their sweethearts.

Soon the Summer Solstice would arrive and the clans would be gathering to celebrate summer, to trade and exchange goods and to visit family members who had married into other clans. The elders of the tribe would have been playing matchmaker and marriages between the clans would be planned and carried out.

Time does not stand still though, and soon it would be time to celebrate and give thanks for the gifts, which have already been bestowed by Mother Earth. Soon it will be time to harvest the plants and make ready again for the approach of winter.

At the Autumn Equinox, the clan is busy gathering plants that have been tended over the summer period. Vegetables, fruits berries and herbs have been prepared for storage for use in the long winter. Meat has been dried, skins cured for clothing and other uses. All too soon winter would be returning. A large bonfire would be lit to show weary travellers the way home before the winter snows would make the journey impossible. A sense of quiet overcomes everyone as they realise that some will survive this winter whilst others will journey to another time, another place.

As the Wheel of the Year makes its final turn, and the Winter Solstice arrives, the clan would celebrate that soon winter would be over and they could once again look forward to spring.

These are the cycles and the teachings that are followed by modern day pagans all over the world and with each turn of the wheel we pagans give thanks to our ancestors who handed down their secrets and rejoice for the season just past and the new one approaching.

Why do People Think That Witches are Bad?

Bad press

Not too long ago if anyone had suspected you of being a witch they would have reported you to the authorities. For just being suspected of witchcraft you would have been burnt at the stake for your crime or, you would have been sealed into a barrel and thrown over a cliff, or perhaps hung from high rafters. Once dead, you were then buried on unhallowed ground.

Macbeth

It is said that it was Shakespeare, in his play *Macbeth*, who stereotyped witches as evil, ugly old hags but he was not the only one. There were many before him who were responsible for this and other accusations against witches.

In the fourth act of Macbeth, the first scene is set on a stormy night with thunder crashing all around. In the middle of the cave stands a cauldron round which stand three witches.

First Witch: Thrice the brinded cat hath mew'd.
   [The striped cat has mewed three times]
Second Witch: Thrice and once the hedge-pig whin'd.
   [The hedgehog whined four times]
Third Witch: Harper cries: 'Tis time, 'tis time.
First Witch: Round about the cauldron go; In the poison'd entrails throw.
   Toad, that under cold stone
   Days and nights hast thirty-one
   Swelter'd venom sleeping got,
   Boil thou first i' the charmed pot.
   [Throw the poisoned entrails into the pot and stir them with the

remains of the toad that has sweated under a rock for thirty days.
Boil the mixture in the cauldron … stirring to prevent it from stick-
ing. Yuck, disgusting!]
All: Double, double, toil and trouble;
Fire burn and cauldron bubble.
[Boil for a good period over a hot fire until it bubbles]
Second Witch: Fillet of a fenny snake,
In the cauldron boil and bake;
Eye of newt, and toe of frog,
Wool of bat, and tongue of dog,
Adder's fork, and blind-worm's sting,
Lizard's leg, and howlet's wing,
For a charm of powerful trouble,
Like a hell-broth boil and bubble.
[Take a fillet of snake caught on the fens, add the eye of a newt and
the toe of a frog, the wool of a bat and the tongue of a dog. Don't
forget the adder's tongue, the sting from a blindworm, the wing of
an owl and a lizard's leg. (Who are they kidding?)]
All: Double, double, toil and trouble;
Fire burn and cauldron bubble.
Third Witch: Scale of dragon, tooth of wolf,
Witch's mummy, maw and gulf
Of the ravin'd salt-sea shark,
Root of hemlock digg'd i' the dark,
Liver of blaspheming Jew,
Gall of goat and slips of yew
Sliver'd in the moon's eclipse,
Nose of Turk and Tartar's lips,
Finger of birth-strangled babe
Ditch-deliver'd by a drab,
Make the gruel thick and slab:
Add thereto a tiger's chaudron,
For the ingredients of our cauldron.
[Add a dragon's skin. A wolf's tooth. The stomach and throat of a
hungry shark. Hemlock root that has been dug up in the dark, the
liver of a Jewish person (in Shakespeare's time there was a lot of
prejudice against Jewish people, even more than now), a goat's gall
bladder and the nose and lips of a Turkish person. Not forgetting a
finger from a stillborn child delivered in a ditch by the roadside by
a whore. Top this lot off with tiger's entrails. (Yeah right!)]
All: Double, double, toil and trouble;
Fire burn and cauldron bubble.

Just ask yourself one question: 'Where would one acquire all these ingredients?' No wonder witches had a bad name!

Salem

Many of you will have read *The Crucible*, by Arthur Miller, possibly when you were at school. It's an allegorical play based on the Salem witchcraft trials between 1692 and 1693, through which Miller was satirising the events of the communist 'witch-hunts' of Senator Joseph McCarthy in the 1950s. But if you read the play on a purely historical level, it's an interesting insight into the hysteria that arose in Salem at that time. Set in a Puritan village in Massachusetts the play begins in the home of Reverend Samuel Parris. Elizabeth, his daughter, had become ill when her father discovered her, her cousin Abigail Williams, and several other local girls, dancing 'like heathens' in the woods.

Various suggestions have been put forward as the real reasons for the girls' behaviour: repressed sexuality, the repression of women, local politics and feuds, or the presence of a cereal disease, known as ergot, in the flour which could have given rise to a form of food poisoning causing hallucinations. A popular and plausible suggestion was that Elizabeth Parris and Abigail Williams had become interested in the occult from stories about voodoo that they had heard from Tituba Indian, a servant who had been brought from Barbados by the Reverend Parris.

Whatever the reason, the girls were happy to go along with the witchcraft theory and point the finger of suspicion at several local women. The hysteria escalated and many more were accused.

Landowner Giles Corey was tortured because he remained silent throughout his indictment, and he was gradually, horrifically crushed to death under a plank of wood weighted with large rocks. In all, nineteen people were executed because of the dubious testimonies of the girls.

Even more were sentenced to death but for various reasons did not actually go to the gallows. The girls felt they were in a position of extreme power and that they could accuse anyone and get away with it. But they were quite wrong. They chose to accuse the wife of the governor, William Phips. This was a step too far and finally Phips dissolved the court that had been trying the supposed witches.

The girls themselves were lucky to escape punishment and didn't show any desire to repent or ask for forgiveness (except for Ann Putnam who, fourteen years later, delivered her half-hearted confession in Salem Church saying she had been deluded by Satan and that the guilt lay with him). Steps of atonement were taken by clergy and state, an Official Day of Humiliation was held in 1697 and the colonial legislature of Massachusetts eventually financially compensated the families of the executed in 1711.

The Paisley witches

The persecution of witches was at its peak in the 14th century and continued for another 300 years, during which time thousands of country folk were tortured, maimed and murdered as witches and Devil worshippers throughout Europe. The following is just one example of hundreds that interested me because it is a story originating from Scotland, in fact, from my own town.

In Paisley in Renfrewshire, a horseshoe is embedded into a major crossroads to mark the spot where witches were hung.

It is recorded that in 1697, an eleven-year-old girl, named Christina Shaw, the daughter of John Shaw of Bargarran, accused her maidservant, with whom she had frequent quarrels, of bewitching her. Christina was reported to have had a spiteful temper. It has also been suggested that she could have been suffering from epilepsy or indeed that the whole thing could have been one big sham.

Her story was believed, unfortunately, and it led to the conviction of over twenty folk from neighbouring villages and parishes throughout Renfrewshire. Paisley Tollbooth, which was demolished in 1897, is where these poor innocents were tried, and seven of the accused were found guilty as charged, condemned to be 'strangled' on the gallows and burnt in a peat fire on the Paisley Green. One of the convicted, 'The Warlock', John Reid was imprisoned in the Renfrew prison where he committed suicide, cheating the executioners and spectators maybe, but adding fuel to their tales of possession and demonology. The talk in the town back in 1697 was that the Devil had come to claim his own. It was said to have been impossible for John Reid to hang himself as he did but that is another story.

The other six, convicted by the word of a mere girl, were indeed marched to the site of execution and paraded through the town to the delight of spectators who had journeyed from as far a-field as Edinburgh for this gruesome spectacle. A very basic set of gallows were set up, and one by one, the six folk were pushed off and hung by their necks and left struggling till they breathed no more. The mortal remains of the poor folk were thrown onto a peat fire and the dirty deed was blown away in the breeze. The spectacle was so shocking that even the lesser-educated people of the day actually questioned the reality of it all. The Minister of one of the local Parishes even called a mass fast to try and incite some forgiveness into this dreadful act.

This trial excited considerable disgust in Scotland. The Rev. Mr Bell, a contemporary writer, observed that, in this business:

'Persons of more goodness and esteem than most of their calumnia-
tors were defamed for witches.' He adds, that the persons chiefly to
blame were 'certain ministers of too much forwardness and absurd
credulity, and some topping professors in and about Glasgow.'

The whole thing was so serious that the horseshoe was solemnly
placed on the site of the gallows. Was this to prevent evil spirits from
seeking revenge on the town for this horrible deed, or was it to serve
as a reminder to the people of Paisley of the tragic crime that their
ancestors had committed?

Christina Shaw grew up to become quite a celebrity in Paisley.
Following her travels around the world she brought various thread-
making skills back to Paisley and created quite a sensation in the
weaving industry. This industry became a major concern in Paisley,
perhaps thanks to Christina Shaw of Bargarran, but at what cost.

As rumours grow and become myths and legends, so the witch trial
became linked to the weaving industry. It was said if the horseshoe
was ever removed that a curse would befall the weaving community.
Another story goes on to say that a young local man on his way back
from his favourite tavern after one or two beers too many thought it
would be amusing to remove the horseshoe. Apparently over the next
few weeks there were about six mysterious suicides among the local
weaving community. The young man was so distressed he turned himself in to the constabulary of the time and confessed his 'prank'. The
horseshoe was returned immediately to its resting-place and indeed it
can be seen there to this very day over 300 years after the witch trials.

The other 16 or so folk who were originally accused, may have
escaped the gallows but records show they were still imprisoned over a
year later, living in very poor conditions, half starving no doubt. Many
people are quite passionate that a memorial of some kind should be
placed in Paisley to formally admonish the accused of 1697.

It was another forty years before the laws changed to prevent such
ridiculous accusations being taken so far and it became illegal to
accuse someone of bewitchment. The repeal of the Witchcraft Act
was passed in 1951.

Good press

In Paisley today you can go into jewellery stores and find pentacles, the
witches' sign, on rings, bracelets and necklaces. Other shops stock all
types of books on Wicca, paganism, spiritual development healing and
magik. Look at the success of the Harry Potter books by J. K. Rowling,
books originally written for children but read and loved by adults
too. *The Secret Garden* by Frances Hodgson Burnett was the first story

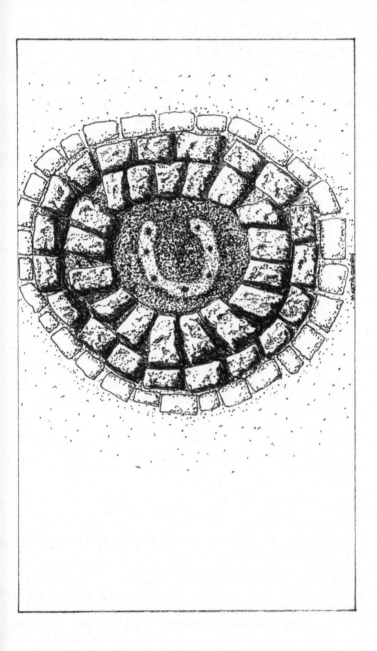

I read as a child that made me see that if you believed in something enough you could really make it happen.

Back in the Sixties, two programmes helped to turn things around and make magik less of a threat and more like entertainment. The first of these was *Bewitched*, with the late Elizabeth Montgomery. The lead character Samantha twitched her nose to make things happen. No matter how hard I tried I could never manage to twitch my nose and my mouth wiggled instead. *I Dream of Genie* with Barbara Eden was my other favourite about a soldier who found a genie in a bottle.

Switch on the television today and you can watch programmes that feature modern-day witches and magik. *Charmed*, *Sabrina the Teenage Witch*, *Buffy the Vampire Slayer*, *Angel* and many children's programmes too.

Films have been made about the Old Craft some of them are quite good whilst others are laughable. *The Craft*, for example is a tale of four college students who possess supernatural powers. Exaggerated of course, but it is one of the best because it does show what can happen when people start dabbling in magik and have no real understanding of the power of their actions. *The Fifth Element* with Bruce Willis is another, and I particularly enjoyed this one because it identified the fifth element as being love.

Misuse of magik

Afternoon radio and television programmes feature all kinds of psychics and one television channel devotes an entire programme to the Mysteries. It is so popular that it runs twice a week. No doubt people are fascinated enough to justify the volume of coverage that these subjects receive and they are all linked in one way or another to Wicca.

People appear on these programmes and declare that they are white witches. Well, what else would they say? Would they be likely to admit that they have taken the other path and practise black magic?

Recently a national daily newspaper produced an article featuring someone claiming to be a witch. The article included a spell for binding someone to you for life. Can you even begin to imagine how terrible that would be?! How often have you heard of a person who has fallen in love with someone and married or lived with that person and then later found them to be violent or abusive?

If you bind someone to you for life, it means life – not only this life but all your lives, for all eternity. Good or bad this is a permanent spell. It can be hard enough getting out of a difficult relationship in one lifetime without having to endure it for infinity.

People change and, with the passage of time, what they want often changes too. Sometimes we meet and fall in love with someone and later we find that the person that we fell in love with is not who we had thought them to be. Under normal circumstances, ideally, you discuss your feelings with this person and either find a way to sort out your differences or find a way to break up the relationship as painlessly as possible. But, if you have been stupid enough to cast a binding spell, or worse, someone else has done this to you, then your problems begin.

We've all heard stories in the press and on television of the misery that can be caused by stalkers. Their compulsive obsessions can create this kind of magik. Not because they have knowledge of magik but probably because they do not understand that the power of their intentions create magik. Good, bad or indifferent, magik is all around us.

Knowing how to use magik for the highest good becomes crucial.

A Magikal Journey

This is not a journey to undertake lightly or just because you are curious. Wicca is a way of life that has been handed down over centuries by our ancestors. This way of life has been given to us to guide us on our path, to show us that everything that we do has a reaction, to teach us that we must honour and respect the world in which we live and the people with whom we share this world, regardless of their race, colour, creed, status, or opinions. This is a high demand. Can you live up to it?

If and when you decide that you are indeed a witch, or, more precisely, a pagan, it will be like the first day of a magical journey. There will be so many questions to ask and so many new things to try. That is when the real task begins because the chances are that you will not know where to begin and who to ask. That is normal. For me this is the Goddess's way of making sure that you are serious in your undertaking. Faint heart falls by the wayside. If it was easy anyone could do it, but it is not easy. The first recognition of how hard it can be is if friends think that you are some sort of weirdo and begin to drift away. Then you may have to endure derisory, ignorant comments from people who do not know what they are talking about, and worse, do not want to know.

You may feel for a time that you are going round in circles, bewildered and insecure, and that is the way that it should be. This is part of your apprenticeship. This is where you begin to understand yourself, your desires, your motives, your fears and your strengths. Overcoming all of this will lead you to your first teacher. In the craft, as we pagans call it, 'When the student is ready the teacher appears'. Teachers are also very aware that students have a lot to teach them too. We all learn and grow from our experiences.

Gradually, you will begin to recognise that you are being drawn towards like-minded people, and them to you, and new friends will be made. Do not, however, be lulled into the assumption that because these new friends are pagans like you that they must be nice. There are nice and not so nice people in the craft too. You will begin to find books that point you in the right direction. You will spend a lot of time on your own studying everything that you can lay your hands on about the mysteries. You will have a deeper understanding of the ever-renewing cycles of birth, life, death, and rebirth.

Do I have to join a coven?

Many people, myself included, prefer to work alone. I do have many students who call, write and e-mail me when they need guidance on their next step or if there is something that they do not understand. My reason for working alone is simple: I like to be in control of my own destiny and what happens in my circle. I also do not have the spare time required to go and meet with other like-minded people. Occasionally though I pine for the sharing that working with others brings.

A coven is simply a group of like-minded people who gather together to practise, learn and celebrate. Traditionally a coven was made up of thirteen people. Immediately you are probably thinking 'spooky', that thirteen is a bad number, but Jesus had twelve apostles so when they gathered to talk and learn or celebrate, they would be thirteen. As a numerologist, which means I have an understanding of the hidden meaning of numbers, the number thirteen for me becomes four, (i.e., 1 + 3) and four is the number of stability and security.

When taking the Wiccan path it is important that you do what is right for you and if you want to work alone then so be it. If however you prefer to work with others then take your time. You must have great respect, admiration and trust for your High Priest or High Priestess. This person, or these people, will be your mentors or guides and they should never abuse you or your trust in them. They too will take their time in getting to know something about you to make sure that they are not letting someone who has unscrupulous motives for choosing a pagan path into their group. That is the way that it should be, for if a coven is eager to accept you without question then they are not discriminating enough about who their members are. This has nothing to do with their sex, colour, or creed. The motives that lie behind the desire to follow a pagan path must be genuine. If the motives of the student and the motives of the coven are true and honourable then they will work well together.

What does a coven do?

Covens meet, to exchange ideas, to talk, to share and to perform rituals. Some rituals are for the purpose of healing those who are sick. This can be generalised to everyone who is suffering from some kind of illness or it can be focused on a more personal level and directed to friends or family known to that group. Some rituals are performed for the benefit of healing Mother Earth, the planet: to ease the wars, famines, oil spills, earthquakes or floods. Covens meet and perform rituals to ease the suffering of the earth, of man, of animals and of plants.

One particularly notable ritual was carried out early in the Second World War. A group of witches gathered on the shores of Britain and performed a ritual to banish the threat of a German invasion and to invoke the safe return of British and allied forces. The Dunkirk evacuation was spread over the period May to June 1940. The British Army were compelled to fall back due to the collapse of their allies the Belgians and French. Initially, only small numbers of men could be evacuated by Royal Naval vessels which were under constant air attack. Sixty-eight thousand troops were rescued on one day by a flotilla of small vessels, channel ferries and Navy war ships. Although the losses were staggering, many were saved. More than 338,000 were rescued. Did this ritual have anything to do with this? We will never know but the power of prayer is a wonderful thing and magik is simply a prayer of a different kind.

The *Collins English Dictionary* describes prayer as 'A personal communication or petition addressed to a deity in the form of supplication, adoration, praise, contrition or thanksgiving'. Almost every faith or religion has some form of prayer. Muslims use a prayer mat to kneel or prostrate themselves whilst praying to their god. Buddhists use a prayer wheel, which is filled with prayers. Each spin of the wheel is likened to these prayers being offered.

A pagan ritual is a form of prayer in the style chosen by the coven to the deity, God and Goddess of the coven.

Do I have to dance naked in the moonlight?

Well ... you can if you want to ... but that will be your decision. In Wicca, some people prefer to work 'sky clad', as we call it, but, to be honest with you, I can't see the necessity for this. When people work with magik and rituals they are working with energy. This energy is so powerful that it can change the course of events. If you believe that to be so then it must follow that this energy must be powerful enough to go through clothing.

The term 'naked and unadorned' is often used in rituals, however, I see this as a metaphor for being stripped of ego. Rituals are performed for the highest good, using pure energy and there is no room here for ego. My ego would have me being too worried about stretch marks and blemishes or prying eyes to concentrate on my tasks so I prefer to work clothed, but some like to work sky clad and that is their choice.

Others like to wear robes or gowns that have been made especially for their circle work (see *Why Cast a Circle?* page 71). It is nice to have something special to wear when you are working in your circle and making your own gown is all part and parcel of making your ritual special. This can be as elaborate or as simple as you like. I found some wonderful fabric in an Asian fabric shop. My name, Soraya, translated means 'the brightest star in the galaxy of seven stars' so you can imagine how thrilled I was to find some vibrant blue silk organza embroidered all over with gold beads in the shape of stars. I have two pieces of this and I use one as an altar cloth and the other as a cape. This is fine for working indoors but something more substantial is required for working outside, especially in cold weather. The Pagan Federation's quarterly magazine, *Pagan Dawn*, often carries advertisements for people who specialise in handmade gowns and robes if you are unable to make your own.

How often do covens meet?

Covens meet as often as they wish to. Some will meet weekly to talk, exchange ideas and plan their celebrations. Others may meet on a monthly basis on, or around, the time of the full moon. The full moon is a special time for pagans and some sort of ceremony will be carried out. They may simply light a candle on their work station or altar and spend a few minutes in quiet meditation or they will perform a ritual ceremony which is known as a Full Moon Esbat.

A working witch will cast a fresh circle every morning and be in or around it for the rest of the day, and magik in any shape or form can be practised at almost any time. There are special times though when circles will be cast even if magik is not being performed. Circles are cast at times of the full moon to honour the cycle of the moon, to honour the goddess or god associated with that time of year and festival, to draw down the power and energy of the moon.

There are eight special festivals during the year when pagans will gather together or work alone to celebrate these special days know as sabbats.

In the Wiccan calendar there are four great sabbats or festivals and four lesser sabbats or festivals. The eight sabbats are:

Imbolc
(Greater Sabbat) which is celebrated on February 2.
Imbolc is known as a festival of light.

The Spring Equinox
(Lesser Sabbat) which is celebrated on March 21.

Beltane
(Greater Sabbat) which is celebrated on April 30.

The Summer Solstice
(Lesser Sabbat) which is celebrated on June 22.

Lammas
(Greater Sabbat) which is celebrated on July 31.

The Autumn Equinox
(Lesser Sabbat) which is celebrated on September 21.

Samhain
(Greater Sabbat) which is celebrated on October 31.

Yule
(Lesser Sabbat) which is celebrated on December 22.

Rituals in the Pagan Tradition

It is not just weddings that are different in pagan tradition. In fact all ceremonies are different whether they be weddings, christenings or funerals. A few of these are outlined below with some explanation regarding the symbolism involved.

How do witches marry?

A handfasting is a pagan wedding and ceremonies vary according to the traditions of different groups or couples. The term handfasting comes from 'hand fastening', and in most ceremonies it is usual to tie the hands of the bride and groom together using cords or ribbons to symbolise their union.

In addition to the ritual of the ceremony, spells for love, passion, fertility, prosperity and continued good health may be included. In a handfasting, the bride and groom represent the God and the Goddess, he is the hunter that provides and she is the mother earth that nurtures and loves. Often when pagans talk of getting married they refer to jumping the broomstick and a handfasting would be incomplete if the bride and groom did not jump over the broom. No matter how solemn the ceremony, it would be difficult to suppress the clapping and cheering at this part of the ceremony. The broom represents binding together male and female aspects. The three parts of the broom are the handle, which is a representation of the male phallus, the bristles represent the female, and the twine is that which binds masculine and feminine together. The broom also sweeps away the old and allows the couple to have a fresh new beginning.

Couples may choose to marry for eternity and that means forever, in this life and in future lives. Other couples may choose to unite 'till death do us part' or they may choose to be united while their love burns strong and sure. They may also choose to be united for a year and a day. At the end of this time they may renew their vows and lengthen the period or separate.

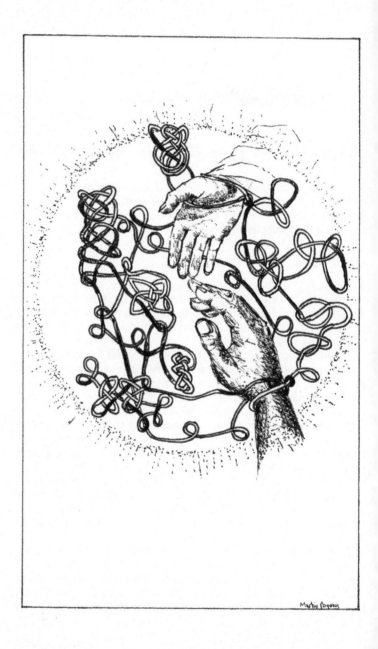

Naming ceremonies

Naming ceremonies are the equivalent of Christenings but more thought is given to the Christening gift than for a conventional ceremony. To begin with, mother witch would have consulted an astrologer to find out her new baby's strengths and weaknesses, based on the child's time date and place of birth and this chart would be used to understand where the child may require extra encouragement. As the time for the naming ceremony approaches, those who will attend will already be thinking of the gifts that they will bestow. These come in the form of blessings. An artist would focus on blessing the child with the gift of creativity. Someone who had a good singing voice or was skilled with a musical instrument would bless the child with the gift of music. Each person would bestow on the child his or her greatest gift. A circle would be cast and each friend or coven member would, one by one, place their hand on the baby and as they did so they would visualise the child being proficient in that skill or talent.

Last rites

Even in death there is celebration and though we witches mourn the passing of a loved one in the flesh we believe in celebrating the passage into another time and dimension. It is traditional for mourners to wear white or pastel shades rather than black, and most pagans prefer to have a woodland burial or, if a cremation is preferred, the ashes may be scattered in a favourite woodland area. A tree is often planted instead of a headstone.

The Cycles

In magik, the cycles are important. Not just the cycles of birth, life, death and rebirth but an hour, a day, a week, a month, a quarter (thirteen weeks) then a year. Sometimes magik can be very quick and a spell can produce a result in an hour. Other spells take time and you may have to wait a month, or even a year.

If we begin our magikal journey with a compass we start at the east, move to the south, the west and lastly the north.

East corresponds to the element of air. Air is the formation of an idea or a thought or a plan.

South corresponds to the element of fire. In the south, we bring energy to our plan.

West corresponds to the element of water. This is where we introduce purity, love and flowing movement to our magik.

North corresponds to the element of earth.

This is where our magik begins to grow and is blessed with abundance. The face of the compass is round reminding us again of the cycles of birth, life, death and rebirth. In Native American traditions, the dream catcher reminds us of this too, formed round the sacred hoop with ancient symbols.

When we are small children we are in the east quarter of our lives and as we grow with knowledge and understanding we move to the south. In our middle age, we are in the west and we move in our old age to the north. Death and rebirth occurs and we begin again in the east.

Invoking rituals

All invoking rituals, where you want to bring something towards you or another person, are performed when the moon is rising. When the

moon is rising, it is called a waxing moon. The waxing moon is the best time to invoke good health, recovery from illness or strife, peace of mind and contentment, protection, romance, and career opportunities.

Banishing rituals

Banishing rituals are performed when the moon is reducing or waning. In a banishing ritual you would send away or repel situations. You would banish illness, disease, anxiety, threats, jealousy, poverty, and loneliness.

The four stages of the moon

There are four stages or quarters to the moon's progress. In the first quarter, the new moon begins to appear first as a tiny sliver and grows in strength each evening. In the second quarter, we can see half of the moon and since we know that it is growing, it is waxing. During the third quarter the moon grows in strength and beauty and becomes full. The fourth quarter is when the moon begins to wane and reduce in size.

The chapter Phases of the Moon, at the end of this book includes the cycles of the moon and indicates when the moon is in a particular sign so that you know when it is best to cast a spell.

The moon and the signs of the zodiac

As you become more aware of the movement and influence of the moon and the planets you will realise that when the moon is in particular planets or signs of the zodiac your magik can be more focused or empowered.

There are times though, when the moon is in between two signs of the zodiac when it is known as being 'void of course'. This is not a good time to perform any kind of magik that demands a certain outcome.

The moon travels round in a cycle, which lasts a little more than twenty-eight days. During this journey, the moon passes through the twelve signs of the zodiac. It remains in each sign for a period of two to three days. It does not appear in one sign and then jump immediately to the next sign. It is a gradual process. During the short period when the moon reaches the point when it is in neither one sign nor the other, unexpected things occur and plans tend to go awry. For that reason, it is best not to perform magikal rites during these times because it is more likely to go wrong.

If you incorporate some knowledge of the qualities of the planets and the signs of the zodiac in planning your working spells you will have greater results. Being aware of the qualities of each sign will help you to choose the best time for any given spell.

Aries ♈ 🐏

Dates: 21st March–20th April
Element: Fire
Quality: Cardinal
Symbol: The ram
Nature: Masculine
Day: Tuesday
Metal: Iron or steel
Gem: Bloodstone
Colour: Red
Occupation: Politics
Governs: The head
Key word: Energy
Positive influences: Courage and action
Negative influences: Greed and destruction
Ruler: Mars, God of War ♂

Taurus ♉ 🐂

Dates: 21st April–20th May
Element: Earth
Quality: Fixed
Symbol: The bull
Nature: Feminine
Day: Friday
Metal: Copper
Gem: Moss agate
Colour: Red and orange
Occupation: Economics
Governs: The ears, neck and throat
Key word: Love
Positive influences: Patience, affection and persistence
Negative influences: Stubbornness, aggression and jealousy
Ruler: Venus, Goddess of Love ♀

Gemini ♊ 👯

Date: 21st May–21st June
Element: Air

Quality: Mutable
Symbol: The twins
Nature: Masculine
Day: Wednesday
Metal: Quicksilver
Gem: Emerald
Colour: Orange
Occupation: Education
Governs: Hands, arms, chest and lungs
Key word: Expression
Positive influences: Affection, intelligence, and astuteness.
Negative influences: Pretentiousness, shallowness and restlessness.
Ruler: Mercury, God of Knowledge ☿

Cancer ♋ ⚹

Date: 22nd June–22nd July
Element: Water
Quality: Cardinal
Symbol: The crab
Nature: Feminine
Day: Friday
Metal: Silver
Gem: Moonstone
Colour: Orange and yellow
Occupation: The land
Governs: The chest and stomach
Key word: Enigmatic
Positive influences: Self-reliant, loyal and kind
Negative influences: Unforgiving, selfish and deep.
Ruler: The Moon, Goddess of Life ☽

Leo ♌ 🦁

Date 23rd July–22nd August
Element: Fire
Quality: Fixed
Symbol: The lion
Nature: Masculine
Day: Sunday
Metal: Gold
Gem: Ruby
Colour: Yellow

Occupation: The arts
Governs: The heart
Key word: Creativity
Positive influences: Considerate, dynamic, and charming
Negative influences: Egotistic, forceful, quick tempered.
Ruler: The Sun, God of Life ○

Virgo ♍ ♎

Date: 23rd August–22nd September
Element: Earth
Quality: Mutable
Symbol: The maiden
Nature: Feminine
Day: Wednesday
Metal: Quicksilver
Gem: Diamond
Colour: Yellow and green
Occupation: Public services
Governs: The digestive organs and the intestine
Key word: Expression
Positive influences: Balanced, organised and courteous
Negative influences: Negative, fretful and exacting
Ruler: Mercury, God of Knowledge ☿

Libra ♎ ♎

Date: 23rd September–22nd October
Element: Air
Quality: Cardinal
Symbol: The scales
Nature: Masculine
Day: Friday
Metal: Copper
Gem: Jasper
Colour: Green
Occupation: Law
Governs: The loins, kidneys and back
Key word: Affection
Positive influences: Charming, refined and affectionate
Negative influences: Cutting, harsh and arrogant
Ruler: Venus, Goddess of Love ♀

Scorpio ♏ 🦂

Date: 23rd October–21st November
Element: Water
Quality: Fixed
Symbol: The scorpion
Nature: Feminine
Day: Tuesday
Metal: Plutonium
Gem: Topaz
Colour: Green and blue
Occupation: Finance
Governs: The reproductive areas
Key word: Transformation
Positive influences: Determined, magnetic and sincere
Negative influences: Challenging, secretive and headstrong.
Ruler: Pluto, God of the Underworld ♇

Sagittarius ♐ 🏹

Date: 22nd November–21st December
Element: Fire
Quality: Mutable
Symbol: The archer
Nature: Masculine
Day: Thursday
Metal: Tin
Gem: Turquoise
Colour: Blue
Occupation: Travel
Governs: The thighs
Key word: Progress
Positive influences: Adventurous, thoughtful and independent
Negative influences: Impulsive, self-centred and domineering
Ruler: Jupiter, God of Fortune ♃

Capricorn ♑ 🐐

Date: 22nd December–19th January
Element: Earth
Quality: Cardinal
Symbol: The goat
Nature: Feminine

Day: Saturday
Metal: Lead
Gem: Lapis
Colour: Deep blue
Occupation: Civil service
Governs: The knees
Key word: Authority
Positive influences: Independent, refined and disciplined
Negative influences: Insecure, critical and proud
Ruler: Saturn, God of Time

Aquarius ♒ ♒

Date: 20th January–18th February
Element: Air
Quality: Fixed
Symbol: The water carrier
Nature: Masculine
Day: Wednesday
Metal: Uranium
Gem: Sapphire
Colour: Indigo
Occupation: Parliament
Governs: The calves and ankles
Key word: Confrontation
Positive influences: Affectionate, modest and intelligent
Negative influences: Judgmental, critical and extreme
Ruler: Uranus, the God of Air

Pisces ♓ ♓

Date: 19th February–20th March
Element: Water
Quality: Mutable
Symbol: The fishes
Nature: Feminine
Day: Friday
Metal: Platinum
Gem: Pearl
Colour: Violet
Occupation: Health care
Governs: The feet
Key word: Inspiration

Positive influences: Intuitive, sensitive and kind
Negative influences: Argumentative, excessive and selfish
Ruler: Neptune, God of the Sea ♅

Preparing Your Magikal Tools

Almost everything that you will need to practise your own magik and to work in a circle you will find in your own home, or it will be easily obtainable or easy to make from equipment that you already have in the home.

A Book of Shadows

The first thing that you must have is a Book of Shadows. Think of this as a homework book. Everything that you learn about in the craft should be written in your Book of Shadows. For this, buy the best that you can afford. When I began, I started with a hardback notebook, but that means transferring all the information into your special book. Some of the things that you may want to write about are spells, when spells were carried out and at what point they achieved a successful outcome, rituals, remedies, supplies and suppliers. It will be your book and it is something very special that can be handed down for generations to come.

Magikal tools

A broom
A wand
An athame (magikal knife)
A bolline (working knife)
A pentacle, the five pointed star
A cauldron
Four candles which are placed at the four quarters
A cup or chalice
A bell
A table or large tray
A mat on which to kneel or sit
A large white altar candle

A large black altar candle
A dinner candle
A small pouring jug filled with water
A small dish of salt
A small empty dish
A small pointed knife
A censer, some incense or smudge sticks
Matches or a lighter
A candle snuff
A towelling cloth, a face cloth is ideal.
Some crystals, if you have them, to place round your working surface

Now that you have assembled your tools, you will want to have some understanding of what they are for and why you would want to use them.

The broom or besom

A besom is a broom, traditionally made using ash for the handle and birch twigs for the brush. They are inexpensive to purchase and can be personalised by carving or painting the handle and adding symbols of your choice. I have several of these, the first one given to me by my children many years ago. Another of my favourites is one that I have decorated with turquoise suede and feathers typical of Native American styles. The besom is used primarily as a purifier, and many Wiccan rituals begin by sweeping the area where the sacred circle is to be cast in order to remove any negative energy. The besom can also be used as a protective implement by laying it under the bed, across a windowsill or across the threshold of your property.

Wand

A wand is used to draw magikal symbols on the ground or in the air, for directing energy, and for calling upon the Goddess. A wand can be made of crystal or a branch from a tree can be used. Each sign of the zodiac is associated with a particular tree so if you would like to have a wand that is compatible with your sign the following information will help you:

Astrological Sign	Tree
Aries	Alder
Taurus	Willow
Gemini	Hawthorn
Cancer	Oak
Leo	Holly
Virgo	Hazel
Libra	Vine
Scorpio	Ivy
Sagittarius	Elder
Capricorn	Birch
Aquarius	Rowan
Pisces	Ash

Athame (magikal knife)

The dagger is used for connecting the energy from the source of infinity above, the sky – the stars and the air – with the source of the energy below, Mother Earth. It is used to direct energy and to open and close doorways to your circle. In Wicca, we would use a traditional dagger, which is called an athame. You can also use a sword, a crystal wand or a small wooden branch taken from a favourite tree. Remember though that a tree, as with any plant, is a living element and some courtesy should be shown here. To remove a branch from a tree, stand quietly in front of the tree and explain the purpose for which the branch is intended. It is also nice to leave a small gift of some fruit or a coin as an offering. Some people use two athames, one for consecrating and sealing the circle and another for working on their altar. I use one for consecrating and closing my circle and I use a large crystal wand for my altar work.

Bolline (working knife)

The knife is usually white handled and is used in the gathering of herbs and plants, cutting wands, and to inscribe symbols into candles when you are using candle magik or for inscribing symbols on to your broom or wand.

Pentacle

A pentacle is an ancient symbol in the shape of a five-pointed star, which has one point at the top, one each to the left and right and two more at the bottom. The top point of the pentacle points to infinity above and, moving clockwise, the next point symbolises water, the next fire, and the next earth and lastly air. The space in the middle is the space that mankind symbolically occupies. A circle symbolising infinity and protection generally surrounds this five-pointed star. Most Wiccans wear a pentacle as a piece of jewellery around their neck or on a ring. Some consider the symbol too sacred to be seen by the eyes of other people and always keep it covered. The choice is yours to do as you wish.

The pentacle is always used in circle work, drawn in the air and placed on the altar and this reminds us of the ever-renewing cycles of balance, life, death and rebirth in all aspects. The pentacle can be used for evoking spirits and calling upon the Goddess. Pentacles can be purchased in most New Age shops but can also be made.

If you have a computer, a simple way to draw one is to open a Microsoft Word document, click on 'insert', and on the drop down menu click on 'picture'. When you have done this a new box titled 'AutoShapes' will appear. Choose the stars and banners icon, click on this, click on the five-pointed star and your pointer on the screen will become a cross. Hold down the left mouse button, press the shift button (this will give you a perfectly proportioned shape) and drag the mouse until the star appears in the size that you want. Print this out and use it as a template to help you draw or paint your own pentacle. If you are artistic, you could even make one from plaster, papier-mache or wire. Your pentacle should be placed on the centre of your altar.

Cauldron

What self-respecting witch would be without a cauldron? However, it took me ages to find mine. I searched high and low, looking in second hand and antique shops and finally I resorted to magik. At the Pagan Federation Annual Conference in Edinburgh I found it. My cauldron's home is in my lounge and a candle burns in it most days. At special times of the year my cauldron is brought outside to my circle and I use it during my rituals. During a full moon it can be filled with water and used for scrying (seeing into the past or the future). Spells can also be created in the cauldron.

Candles

Four candles are placed, one at each of the four quarters, the east, the south, the west and the north, on the outside rim of the circle. You can use tea lights or altar candles for this. In addition to these candles you will need a good supply of a variety of candles in different shapes, sizes and colours. I buy mine in bulk and make some too. When I am working with candle magik I save the end pieces and recycle them, losing none of the power and energy that I have been working with.

Cup or chalice

The cup or chalice is used for symbolically joining the male and female aspects. The cup is feminine and the athame is masculine. At the end of a ritual you would drink your water, wine or fresh juice from the chalice. If you can afford to splash out you can buy one made of silver, brass or gold or you may already have something suitable.

Bell

Ringing a bell will purify and clear the air or the energy around you and, as a feminine object, the bell can be used to call the Goddess. Any bell can be used but the finer the peel the better. I found my bell in a second hand shop. It is made of Caithness glass and has a beautiful sound.

A tray

A large tray is required to carry your tools to your circle, whether you are working inside or out, and this can be used as your work surface if you do not have a table. In Wicca, your work surface would be called an altar. There is nothing sacred about an altar but the purpose for which it is used is sacred. For this reason, many Wiccans will keep their table or tray in their magikal cupboard away from prying eyes or, more aptly, negative vibrations. Each time it is brought out for use it would be carefully washed and blessed for its value and purpose.

A censer or incense stick and burner

Censers can be quite elaborate and expensive but if you pop into any hardware store or gift shop you should be able to find a small brass hanging-plant potholder complete with chains. Put some salt or sand in the bottom, add a charcoal disc which can be purchased from most New Age shops and, when it is white hot, herbs and grains of crystallised gums can be sprinkled on top. This makes it easy to carry around your circle when you are invoking the element of air. If you find it difficult to obtain the loose incense you can use an incense cone or stick instead. This represents the element of air and should be placed at the east section of your table. If you prefer you can substitute a smudge stick instead. Again these can be purchased from any good New Age shop or you can make your own smudge sticks by drying your favourite herbs and then binding them together in a bunch with some twine.

They can be difficult to use initially because after lighting them it is important to blow on them and fan them to create the smoke. It is also important that they are extinguished properly. I use a small pottery jar half filled with salt and when I am finished I place the glowing end of the smudge stick into the salt and press it down firmly. If you are working indoors remember to check it later to ensure that it has gone out.

Other objects

A **table** to use as your altar.

A **mat** comes in handy for kneeling or sitting on, especially if you are working outside. I use a prayer mat purchased from an Asian store. I remember when I went into the shop to buy it the salesman was not going to let me have it. He asked me if I knew what it was and what it was used for. I managed to convince him that it would be used for a good purpose.

One large **white altar candle** is placed on the left of the altar to symbolise the feminine element, the Goddess. You can use a green candle instead.

One large **black altar candle** is placed on the right of the altar to symbolise the masculine element, the God. You can use a red candle instead. These two candles represent balance and harmony just the same as is seen in the yin and yang symbol.

One **dinner candle**, representing the element of fire, should be placed at the south section of your table.

One small pouring **jug** filled with water, representing the element of water, should be placed at the west section of your table.

One small **dish of salt** representing the element of earth should be placed at the north section of your table.

One small **empty dish** should be placed within your reach in front of you to use for blending water and salt during your ceremony.

Your **matches** or **lighter** and **candle snuff** to put out your candles.

Do not forget: never, ever blow your candles out or you will undo all your work.

The **towelling cloth** is important for cleaning your hands especially if you are using essential oils for anointing candles. If you like working with **crystals** or just like having them around you, you can scatter these around your altar.

Why Cast a Circle?

Most rituals take place within a magik or sacred circle. Whilst working within the circle we are between this world and the astral world. It can be likened to meditating. There are guidelines for laying out a magic circle but they are not always necessary. Traditionally, a circle would be 9 feet (2.74 metres) in diameter and a sacred ceremonial chord, which measures 4 feet 6 inches in length (1.37 metres), would be used to measure this. However larger circles would be used for groups performing outdoor rituals and smaller circles may be used if you are working in a tiny space at home.

The most important thing that you can do though, is to prepare your ritual in advance so that you have everything that you need and know exactly what you are doing before you begin. It is not a good idea to break your concentration in the middle of a ceremony in order to go and get something that you have forgotten. This would be considered as an insult to the Goddess and it would also allow negative feelings or energy to enter your sacred space.

A circle is cast to keep the energy pure and focused. Part of this focus is a personal one. If I am working and do not wish to be disturbed, I close my office door so that my concentration is not broken. In my circle, I do the same. Once I am in my sacred space I do not wish to be interrupted or distracted by anyone and I will not stop what I am doing for a telephone call or a visitor at the door. The other reason that I cast a circle is that I do not want negative energy coming into my space. I consider negative energy to be that energy which is created by negative thoughts, deeds, words or actions. If you have just cleaned the carpet in your lounge because you are expecting important guests then you do not want your dog running over it with muddy paws, so you close the door. If this were to happen, by the time your guests had arrived you would be in an apologetic mood and it could spoil the occasion. It is as simple as that.

When you begin to do your work, you will do so in a specific fashion.

If you work in an office, the first thing that you would attend to would probably be the mail and telephone messages. You might then finish tasks that were unfinished before you went home the previous evening. Every day you do the same job and more often than not in the same fashion.

Circle magic has an orderly pattern too. This can be done in the home, the garden, or in your own favourite location.

Working outside is more difficult though. The weather is the first disadvantage. No one wants to work in the pouring rain and it is difficult to light candles when your matches are wet, or when the wind is blowing so fiercely that your candles are blown out. Another disadvantage when working outside is the presence of people out walking, perhaps with their dogs or children. I love dogs and children but I do not want to be distracted by them when I am working.

My favourite place to work is in my home but if the weather is fine, I have a special place in my little garden with some large stones placed round the edge of my circle.

I remember the day that my garden circle was created. The back garden was overgrown with couch grass, weeds and was full of debris. No work had ever been done on it. My partner Martin and I were surveying the overgrown mess and Martin asked what I would like done with it. I closed my eyes and pictured the scene: a special place where I could sit and meditate surrounded by wild flowers and herbs. I made a few suggestions of how I imagined it and thought no more about it. The next day I left early in the morning for a business meeting in Perth. The sun was shining and it was a beautiful day. Much later, when I came home, I was busy chatting to Martin about how my day had gone. I asked him what he had been doing all day and he told me that he had been sitting in the garden. The sun was still shining so we made some tea and took it outside to enjoy the last of the fine day and relax before dinner. I could not believe my eyes when I walked round the house.

Martin had cleared the overgrown jungle and had created a split-level garden. My Buddhas and Chinese lanterns were placed in among shrubs that he had transplanted and he had cleared and re-turfed a circle around which he had placed large boulders. At either side of the entrance to my new circle stood two large planters filled with lavender. I was so excited and touched by the effort that he had made to create my dream that I cried. Martin was happy too and eager to show me all that he had done. When we looked at the stones in my circle we were amazed to discover that each quarter of the circle had a stone which was perfectly placed for due east, south, west and north. Now that is what I call magik!

Preparation

If you are going to work outside the first step is to cast your circle. In traditional circle casting, a broom would be used to sweep round the circle sweeping it clean. A broom can be used to measure the distance of the circle. If you would like to try this then lay the broom on its side with the bristles to the centre of the circle. Place one stone at the bristle end and another at the spot where the end of the handle rests. Moving to the opposite end of the circle and repeating this process would give the diameter. This process would be repeated twice more just like quartering a giant cake. This circle would now have four quarters. The first quarter is the east, the second quarter is south, the third quarter is west and the fourth quarter is north. You can now place stones in the spaces between your quarter stones and there you have it, your own circle.

At this point you must begin to prepare yourself and you do this as you would for any other important event in your life. You can start with a warm bath with essential oils to prepare your mood. My favourites for any kind of spiritual work are marjoram and frankincense.

A nice way to prepare is to lay out the clothes that you have decided to wear and any jewellery that has special meaning to you. Place four small tea light candles at each corner of your bath and light them, starting with the candle at the front left edge of your bath. Then light the furthest left, the furthest right and the front right candle last.

Turn the water on to fill your bath and as the water is running add a few drops of your favourite oil. Next take some sea salt and beginning at the left of your bath sprinkle the salt into the water in a figure-of-eight movement. When the temperature of the water is as you like it, place some of your favourite crystals into the water, turn out the bathroom lights and step into your bath.

While you are lying there go over in your mind those tasks that you are about to perform in your circle. Focus your attention on the energies of the salt, the water and the crystals and feel these energies cleansing and purifying your mind, body and spirit. Finish with a short meditation of your choice.

When you are ready, step out of the bath and then remove the plug and allow the water to drain away. As the water drains away it will remove any negative energy. Do not remove the plug before you are out of the bath or you will drain away all the good energy that you have invoked into your body.

Finally rinse your crystals in clean water. Both you and your circle have now been prepared and you can begin to place all your magikal tools on your altar and set your quarter candles in place.

Casting a circle

Starting at the east, then west, then south and then north, place one small, white candle in each quarter. The sun sets in the west and rises in the east but if you are still unsure of the direction then place the east candle to your left as you face your working surface which is in the centre of your sacred space or circle.

Once this has been done, stand at the edge of your circle and visualise white light pouring into it from infinity above. The best time is when the moon is full and moonlight blesses the circle. Focus your mind on the source of infinity above you, Father God, and the strength of the earth beneath your feet, Mother Earth. I prepare myself spiritually and mentally and think of my intentions. Visualise a temple of light and love growing over your circle. When you are ready, say these words.

The circle is about to be cast and the temple erected.

Let the light and the love and the energy which fills my sacred space be pure and work for the highest good and harm none.

Enter your circle and walk to the altar, and, taking your lighter or matches, light first the large white altar candle then the large black altar candle and lastly the dinner candle. Remove the dinner candle from its holder and move to the east of your circle. Light the east candle from the dinner candle and as you do so say these words:

May the watchtower of the east be blessed with light and air to illuminate this temple and bring it life.

Light the south candle from the dinner candle and as you do so say these words:

May the watchtower of the south be blessed with light and fire to illuminate this temple and bring it warmth.

Light the west candle from the dinner candle and as you do so say these words:

May the watchtower of the west be blessed with light and water to illuminate this temple and wash it clean.

Light the north candle from the dinner candle and as you do so say these words:

May the watchtower of the north be blessed with light and earth to illuminate this temple and bring it strength.

Returning to your altar replace the candle in its holder and pick up the athame. Hold it high above your head with your arms at full stretch. Face the moon and ask again for the blessings from infinity above you. You may feel the energy beginning to course down through your arms. Lower your arms and walk to the east quarter of your circle. Point the athame to the ground and begin to walk round the edge of your circle visualising that you are drawing a golden white line of light with the point of your athame.

Starting at the east, move to the south, then the west, then the north, and back to the east. Move back to where you entered your circle and place the point of the blade into the ground where it will remain until you are ready to finish. If you are working inside your house, you can lay your athame across the entrance to your circle.

Returning to your altar, put your index finger into the container of salt and, as you do so, visualise light energy flowing down through your arm into your hand and into the salt and say these words:

Let this salt of life purify my body and spirit that I may use it for the highest good.

Place three pinches of salt into the water and stir it clockwise three times.

Return to the east rim of your circle and begin to sprinkle the salt and water round the edge of your circle saying as you do so:

I bless the east with salt and water to purify, cleanse and protect my circle.

I bless the south with salt and water to purify, cleanse and protect my circle.

I bless the west with salt and water to purify, cleanse and protect my circle.

I bless the north with salt and water to purify, cleanse and protect my circle.

Move to the east to complete the circle and then return to your altar. Place your dish on the altar and pick up your incense and then say:

I bless the east with this sacred scent to purify, cleanse and protect my circle.

I bless the south with this sacred scent to purify, cleanse and protect my circle.

I bless the west with this sacred scent to purify, cleanse and protect my circle.

I bless the north with this sacred scent to purify, cleanse and protect my circle.

Move to the east to complete the circle and then return to the centre of your circle and place your incense on the altar.

Draw an invoking pentacle

Return to the east edge of your circle and using your athame, crystal, or your index finger, draw an invoking pentacle in the air at the east quarter as you say these words:

May the watchtower of the east, element of air, guard and protect this sacred space and grant me the blessings I require to fulfil my desires so that they harm none.

May the watchtower of the south, element of fire, guard and protect this sacred space and grant me the blessings I require to fulfil my desires so that they harm none.

May the watchtower of the west, element of water, guard and protect this sacred space and grant me the blessings I require to fulfil my desires so that they harm none.

May the watchtower of the north, element of earth, guard and protect this sacred space and grant me the blessings I require to fulfil my desires so that they harm none.

Move to the east to complete the circle and then return to your altar and draw an invoking pentacle above you.

Drawing down the moon

Ring the bell three times and replace it on your altar. Open your arms

wide, raise your hands high above your head, focus all your attention on the moon above you, and visualise the Goddess sending down her light and love to you (see the illustration on the page 69). Draw this energy into your heart, into your spirit and into your body. Give thanks for those blessings that you have already received, your health, your career, your family and your loved ones. Lower your arms and extend them out by your sides saying:

> I call upon the Goddess to ask for assistance with my task. May she be ever-present in my work and in my life.

> I am grateful for those gifts and blessings that I have already been given and I am open and ready to receive those that are waiting to come to me.

This is known as 'drawing down the moon'. What we are really doing here is drawing on the energy of the moon to bring our energy into contact with the energy of the Moon Goddess, restoring our vitality and strengthening our purpose.

Pick up the cup of juice, wine or water and hold it high above your head allowing the energy and the blessings of the moon to charge this liquid. Place the cup on the table, raise the second athame or crystal wand high above your head, and allow the energy and the blessings of the moon to charge it too. Now lower the athame or crystal wand into the cup to symbolise the joining of male and female aspects of deity, of man and of life. Say these words:

> May man and woman be joined for eternal joy and happiness. May the plants that sustain us be fruitful and may we all be blessed with abundance.

Remove the athame from the cup and lay it to one side.

Your circle is now fully charged and you are ready to begin whatever task you have chosen to do.

You can now begin to perform any of the spells contained in this book or any other work that you have decided to do. When you have finished, give the water and salt back to the earth by pouring it into the ground just before you close your circle. If you are working inside your home, you can save this until you have finished and then go outside and pour this sacred liquid on to the soil in your circle or special place. Before you close your circle, say these words:

> Lord and Lady thank you for assisting me with my tasks. We

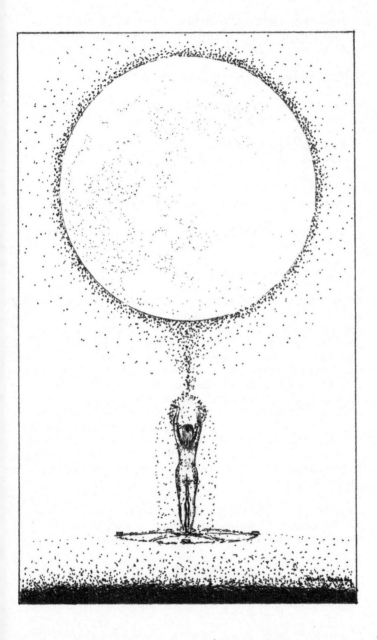

have met in love and friendship, let us part the same way.
May the love that has been in this circle be shared with all.
Merry we meet, merry we part, merry may we meet again.

The temple will now be closed.

May the watchtower of the east, element of air take for your
use any powers that have not been used.

May the watchtower of the south, element of fire, take for
your use any powers that have not been used.

May the watchtower of the west, element of water, take for
your use any powers that have not been used.

May the watchtower of the north, element of earth, take for
your use any powers that have not been used.

And it harm none so mote it be.

Go back to the centre of your circle and begin to clean and clear away
your magikal tools. Take the incense stick and touch it to the liquid
to put it out and give thanks to the element of air for its blessings. If
you are outside, give the sacred liquid back to the earth by pouring it
on the ground. As you do so give thanks to the elements of water and
earth for their blessings.

Using a candle snuff, put out the candles on your altar and, as you
do so, give thanks to the element of fire for its blessings.

Move to the edge of your circle and, using the candle snuff, put out
your candles, one by one, starting at the east quarter, then the south,
the west and lastly the north.

If you have placed your athame in the ground, pick it up now, thank
it for guarding the entrance to your sacred space, and place it with
the rest of your tools.

Rituals or ceremonies are times for celebration and if you are working in a coven you will find that the atmosphere is friendly and happy.
There may be feasting, dancing, singing and storytelling. Obviously
this is not possible if you are working on your own.

part two:

making the magik happen

Singed Knees and Waxy Fingers

This chapter heading came directly from the subject line in an e-mail from one of my students. She was at that time quite worried and depressed about the way things were going in her life and I suggested that she conjure up a few changes. I instructed her on how to cast a circle and do a simple candle magik spell. The e-mail in question was sent to me after her first attempt. She had set out her favourite rug in the middle of the floor in her lounge, set up her candles and began to work her magik. She told me in her e-mail that apart from getting covered in melted wax and singeing both her knees and her favourite rug, she felt much better. Even though the spell had not had time to take effect she felt as though she had done something positive ... but she was lucky that she didn't burn the house down.

Bear this in mind when you begin to practise and remember that, in more ways than one, you can burn your fingers when playing with fire.

Now that you know a little of the background it is time to get down to the nitty gritty. The good news is that magik can be performed anywhere and at any time without too much bother. You can set up a circle around yourself in your mind by visualising your circle around you, complete with all the elements in place and just silently declare the words that are necessary for your chosen spell. This is not as much fun but it is very effective in emergencies or when you are away from home.

All rituals are basically the same, however, the oils, herbs, symbols or colours used for specific spells will be different. There is nothing worse though when preparing to work a spell than having the scene set, complete with your book open at the appropriate page, and then being told to follow the instructions on a different page. So, in this book, my spells include details of everything you will need to gather around you, say and do in each case.

Before you begin to work with your chosen spell you must prepare all your ingredients. Have everything that you need on your workspace or altar and you will feel more confident. This confidence will help you to have successful outcomes to all your spells.

There are spells for every conceivable situation but most people are at some time or another concerned about:

Health

When you or a loved one is ill.

Love

When you or someone close to you feels lonely and unloved. Remember when you are using love spells that you should never try to force a relationship with a particular person.

Career

When you are looking for promotion or securing the best job. Of course there is no point in performing a spell if you do not intend to scan the employment pages and apply for positions! Magic will assist your efforts but you must make that effort in the first place.

Finances

When you need to improve or encourage financial security. No matter how well off you are, at certain times money just seems to stop flowing. There could be a delay, for any number of reasons, in money coming to you that you expect or depend on and an appropriate spell will speed up the arrival and help you to meet your financial obligations.

Protection

When we are affected by negative energies caused by abusive people, situations or even stalkers, a protection spell can act like the knight in shining armour that is so vital to make us feel safe and secure.

Never under any circumstances interfere with someone's will.

Magikal ingredients

Decide first on the spell that you are planning to create and then choose from the lists of ingredients at the beginning of each chapter those items that are easily accessible to you. Remember that you do not need every single item but the more you have the better.

You can vary the times, dates and Goddesses and use your favourites. This list is only a guide to help you initially. Later your magik will become spontaneous and much more fun.

The methods and rituals are explained step by step for each spell. Everything you need to know about each particular spell is contained within each chapter so that you don't have to refer back and forth to other sections.

Now let's make some magik happen!

1 Good Luck

Day of the week: The best day of the week is Thursday

Time of day: The best time of day is 5am. Also noon, 7pm or at any time in the evening when the moon is waxing or full but not when it is waning

God: Quirinus

Goddess: Gamelia

Planet: Jupiter

Guardian Angel: Zadkiel

Star sign: Sagittarius

Metal: Tin, silver or gold

Colour: Blue

Rune: Daeg (also known as Dagaz)

Symbol: Two-sided objects such as coins

Number: Your own birth number. Add together the day, month and year of your birth. [e.g., my date of birth is 25/12/1947 and my birth number is 4. 2+5+1+2+1+9+4+7 = 31, then (3+1) = 4.]

Crystal: Citrine or amber

Flower: White heather

Essential oil: Sandalwood

Herb: Clover

Tree: Cedar

Sagittarius

Jupiter

Daeg

Good luck spell 1

Prepare yourself and decorate your work surface or altar space with all your chosen ingredients such as:

One blue taper candle
One white taper candle
A candle snuff
Several two-sided objects such as coins
A sprig of white heather
A sprig of clover (plants available in garden centres)
An item of silver or gold jewellery
A piece of citrine or amber
A piece of paper with a drawing of the symbol Daeg and the
    number that represents your date of birth.
An ashtray or a small fireproof dish for spent matches or
    any paper that you may light during your spell and some
    matches or a lighter.

When everything is in place, close your eyes and, as you breathe in, visualise positive, white, light energy filling your body. As you breathe out, breathe away all negative energy. After some minutes, you will feel all tension flowing away from your mind and body. Allow pure light energy to flow into and through your entire body filling your sacred space, filling your room. When you are completely relaxed, stand up and move quietly to the east quarter of your circle or room.

Light the east candle and say:
    May the element of air bless this space with light, love and
    air and grant me good fortune.

Light the south candle and say:
    May the element of fire bless this space with light, love and
    fire and grant me good fortune.

Light the west candle and say:
    May the element of water bless this space with light, love
    and water and grant me good fortune.

Light the north candle and say:
    May the element of earth bless this space with light, love
    and earth and grant me good fortune.

Move quietly back to your workspace and kneel in front of your table. Light your white altar candle and meditate quietly on your heart's desire and visualise before you your wish coming true. In your mind, focus on your desire and ask Quirinus and Gamelia to grant you their blessings for good luck. Visualise the Guardian Angel Zadkiel protecting you and surrounding you with good fortune.

Light your blue candle and take your piece of paper and light it from the altar candle and let it burn in the ashtray or small dish.

As it burns say these words:

> Good luck be with me every day.
> Quirinus and Gamelia, hear me pray.
> Zadkiel bring good news,
> Change my fortune that I may not lose.
> And it harm none so be it.

Spend some quiet time in your circle focusing your mind on your luck changing and improving. If you can, allow your altar candle to burn through to the end, but, if you must put it out, do so with a candle snuff or pinch the wick between dampened fingertips.

When you are finished working move quietly to the left of your circle.

Extinguish the east candle and say:
> I thank the element of air for blessing me with good fortune.

Extinguish the south candle and say:
> I thank the element of fire for blessing me with good fortune.

Extinguish the west candle and say:
> I thank the element of water for blessing me with good fortune.

Extinguish the north candle and say:
> I thank the element of earth for blessing me with good fortune.

Close your circle by saying:
> May the four powers give back to the universe any powers and energies that have not been used.
> The work is now done and the circle is closed.
> So mote it be.

Good luck spell 2

10 mls base oil (sunflower, jojoba or almond)
Sandalwood pure essential oil
A bottle for your oil mixture
A small face cloth or some tissues (to clean your hands after
    working with the oil)
An ornament or picture of a black cat
Some citrine or amber, or your favourite crystal
Any items that you consider to be your lucky charms
One tall blue taper candle and holder
One tall white taper candle and holder
One small pointed knife
A small fireproof dish or an ashtray for spent matches or
    any paper that you may light during your spell and some
    matches or a lighter

Prepare a blend of oil using 10 mls of base oil and add three drops of
sandalwood pure essential oil. Hold the bottle of oil in your hands in
the prayer position and rub the bottle vigorously between the palms
of your hands and as you do so visualise the oil being empowered
with good fortune. When you feel as though the oil has been charged,
place it on your altar or work surface ready for use along with the
other ingredients.

Place four small candles at the east, south, west and north, in that
order. When everything is in place, sit or kneel comfortably in front
of your table.

Close your eyes and, as you breathe in, picture positive, white, light
energy filling your body. As you breathe out, breathe away all negative energy. After some minutes, you will feel all tension flowing away
from your mind and body.

Allow pure light energy to flow into and through your entire body
filling your sacred space, filling your room. When you are completely
relaxed stand up and move quietly to the east quarter of your room.

Light the east candle and say:
    *May the element of air bless this space with light, love and
    air and grant me good fortune.*

Light the south candle and say:
    *May the element of fire bless this space with light, love and
    fire and grant me good fortune.*

Light the west candle and say:
> May the element of water bless this space with light, love and water and grant me good fortune.

Light the north candle and say:
> May the element of earth bless this space with light, love and earth and grant me good fortune.

Move quietly back to your workspace and kneel in front of your table. Light your white altar candle and meditate quietly on your heart's desire and visualise your wish coming true. Take your blue spell candle and the small pointed knife and inscribe your lucky number and the rune symbol Daeg at the top of the candle.

Place the candle back in the holder and, taking the bottle of empowered oil, place some in the palm of your hands. Rub your hands together and visualise that you are charging the energy in the oil and in your hands. Your hands will begin to feel very warm.

At this point take the blue spell candle and spread the oil from middle to top and middle to bottom of the candle until the candle is completely covered in oil. While you are doing this visualise that you are empowering the candle with your desire. Keep thinking about your heartfelt desire and whilst doing this rub your hands vigorously together with the candle still held between the palms of your hands. After a few minutes, place your candle back in its holder and light the flame and say these words:

> Candle burning, burning bright,
> Change my luck this very night.
> Bring to me my heart's desire,
> Powered by this magik fire.
> And it harm none so be it.

Allow your candle to burn for as long as possible but if you must put it out do not blow it out otherwise you will reverse or negate your spell. You can use a candle-snuff or pinch the flame between your thumb and finger. You may light your candle again but, each time you do so, visualise your wish as though it has already begun to happen. When you are finished working, clean your hands on the cloth and move quietly to the left of your room.

Extinguish the east candle and say:
> I thank the element of air for blessing me with good fortune.

Extinguish the south candle and say:
  I thank the element of fire for blessing me with good fortune.

Extinguish the west candle and say:
  I thank the element of water for blessing me with good fortune.

Extinguish the north candle and say:
  I thank the element of earth for blessing me with good fortune.

Close your circle by saying:
  May the four powers give back to the universe any powers and energies that have not been used.
  The work is now done and the circle is closed.
  So mote it be.

2 Prosperity

Day of the week: The best day of the week is Sunday
Time of day: The best time of day is 5am. Also noon, 7pm or at any time in the evening when the moon is waxing or full but not when it is waning
Goddess: Aditi
Planet: The sun
Guardian Angel: Michael
Star sign: Leo
Metal: Gold
Colour: Yellow
Rune: Feoh (also known as Fehu)
Symbol: Coal, salt, money or keys
Number: Nine
Crystal: Diamond, jade or ruby
Flower: Sunflower
Essential oil: Rose otto
Herb: Bay
Tree: Cherry

The Sun

Leo

Feoh

Prosperity spell 1

Prepare yourself and decorate your work surface or altar space with all your chosen ingredients such as:

Items of gold and silver
One yellow taper candle
One white taper candle
One piece of coal
A dish of salt
A dish of coins
A key or bunch of keys
Diamond, jade or ruby jewellery
Your purse, wallet or bankbook, even if they are empty
A piece of paper and a pen or pencil
An ashtray or a small fireproof dish for spent matches or
    any paper that you may light during your spell and some
    matches or a lighter

First bathe in a warm luxurious bath to which you have added three drops of rose otto essential oil. Dry yourself with your favourite towel and dab a little of your desired scent on your wrists, behind your ears and over your heart. Dress in your best clothes and, when you are ready and everything is in place, stand at the edge of your circle. Close your eyes and breathe in, visualising light energy filling your body. Breathe out and breathe away all negative energy.

When you are completely relaxed, stand up and move quietly to the east quarter of your circle or room.

Light the east candle and say:
    May the element of air bless this space with light, love and
    air and grant me prosperity.

Light the south candle and say:
    May the element of fire bless this space with light, love and
    fire and grant me prosperity.

Light the west candle and say:
    May the element of water bless this space with light, love
    and water and grant me prosperity.

Light the north candle and say:

May the element of earth bless this space with light, love and earth and grant me prosperity.

Move quietly back to your workspace and kneel in front of your table. Light your white altar candle and meditate quietly on your financial situation as it is now. In your mind see yourself depositing money in your savings account. Your vision should be a happy one where anyone you see is smiling warmly at you. Now see yourself paying all your bills one by one. Having paid all your bills, see yourself buying a special treat for yourself or someone that you care for.

Light your yellow taper candle and as the flame grows write down a sensible sum of money that will make all these things possible. Do not be greedy by asking for the impossible.

Take your piece of paper and light it from the yellow taper candle placing it in the ashtray to burn through. See the smoke from your burning paper carry your wishes to the Goddess Aditi.

In your mind's eye see the rays of the sun surrounding you with abundance and say a prayer in your own words to the Guardian Angel Michael. Stand in front of your altar, raise your hands high above your head and say these words:

> *Coins that sparkle in the sun*
> *Come to me when work is done.*
> *Make me richer by the day,*
> *Wealth aplenty comes my way.*
> *And it harm none so be it.*

Spend some quiet time in your circle focusing your mind on your situation improving. If you can, allow your altar candle to burn through to the end but if you must put it out do so with a candle snuff or pinch the wick between dampened fingertips. When you are finished working move quietly to the left of your circle.

Extinguish the east candle and say:
   I thank the element of air for blessing me with prosperity.

Extinguish the south candle and say:
   I thank the element of fire for blessing me with prosperity.

Extinguish the west candle and say:
   I thank the element of water for blessing me with prosperity.

Extinguish the north candle and say:
  I thank the element of earth for blessing me with prosperity.

Close your circle by saying:
  May the four powers give back to the universe any powers
  and energies that have not been used.
  The work is now done and the circle is closed.
  So mote it be.

Prosperity spell 2

10 mls base oil (such as sunflower, jojoba, or almond)
Rose essential oil
A bottle for your oil mixture
A small face cloth or some tissues (to clean your hands after
    working with the oil)
A precious ornament or picture
Your favourite crystal or most valuable piece of jewellery
Any items of gold or silver
One tall white candle and one gold or silver taper candle and
    holders
One small pointed knife
An ashtray or a small fireproof dish for spent matches or
    any paper that you may light during your spell and some
    matches or a lighter.

Prepare a blend of oils using 10 mls of sunflower oil and add three drops
of rose essential oil. Hold the bottle of oil in your hands in the prayer
position, rub the bottle vigorously between the palms of your hands
and as you do so visualise the oil being empowered with good fortune.
When you feel as though the oil has been charged, place it on your
altar or work surface ready for use along with the other ingredients.

  When everything is in place, put four small candles at the east,
south, west and north in that order. Sit or kneel comfortably in front
of your table.

  Close your eyes and, as you breathe in, picture positive, white light
energy filling your body. When you are completely relaxed, stand up
and move quietly to the east quarter of your room.

Light the east candle and say:
  *May the element of air bless this space with light, love and
  air and grant me abundance.*

Light the south candle and say:
  *May the element of fire bless this space with light, love and
  fire and grant me abundance.*

Light the west candle and say:
  *May the element of water bless this space with light, love
  and water and grant me abundance.*

Light the north candle and say:
  *May the element of earth bless this space with light, love
  and earth and grant me abundance.*

Move quietly back to your workspace and kneel in front of your table.
Light your white altar candle and meditate quietly on your heart's
desire and visualise your wish coming true.

Take your gold or silver spell candle and the small pointed knife
and inscribe the number nine and the rune symbol Feoh at the top
of the candle.

Place the candle back in the holder and, taking the bottle of empowered oil, place some in the palm of your hands. Rub your hands together
and visualise that you are charging the energy in the oil and in your
hands. Your hands will begin to feel very warm. Take the spell candle
and spread the oil from middle to top and middle to bottom of the
candle until the candle is completely covered in oil. Visualise that you
are empowering the candle with your desire. Rub your hands vigorously together with the candle still held between the palms of your
hands. After a few minutes, place your candle back in its holder, light
the flame and say these words:

> As sure as the cherry blossoms in spring
> Aditi and Geb to me wealth bring.
> No more struggle, no more strife,
> By your power enrich my life.
> And it harm none so be it.

Allow your candle to burn for as long as possible, but, if you must put it
out, do not blow it out otherwise you will reverse or negate your spell.
You can use a candle snuff or pinch the flame between your thumb
and finger. You may light your candle again but, each time you do so,

visualise your wish as though it has already begun to happen. When you are finished working, clean your hands on the cloth and move quietly to the left of your room.
Extinguish the east candle and say:
   I thank the element of air for blessing me with abundance.

Extinguish the south candle and say:
   I thank the element of fire for blessing me with abundance.

Extinguish the west candle and say:
   I thank the element of water for blessing me with abundance.

Extinguish the north candle and say:
   I thank the element of earth for blessing me with abundance.

Close your circle by saying:
   May the four powers give back to the universe any powers and energies that have not been used.
   The work is now done and the circle is closed.
   So mote it be.

3 Gratitude

Day of the week: The best day of the week is Monday

Time of day: The best time of day is 5am. Also noon, 7pm or at any time in the evening when the moon is waxing or full but not when it is waning

Goddess: Rangda

Planet: Moon

Guardian Angel: Gabriel

Star sign: Pisces

Metal: Silver

Colour: White

Rune: Ken (sometimes known as Kano or Kenaz)

Symbol: Circular objects and fruit

Number: Three

Crystal: Snow quartz or opal

Flower: Hibiscus

Essential oil: Bergamot

Herb: Saffron

Tree: Birch

Moon

Pisces

Ken

Gratitude spell 1

Prepare yourself and decorate your work surface or altar space with
all your chosen ingredients such as:

Any silver items
One silver and one white taper candle
A posy of white flowers
A bowl of fruits
A dish of coins
A piece of snow quartz

When you are ready and everything is in place, stand at the edge of
your circle. Close your eyes and breathe in, visualising light energy
filling your body. Breathe out and breathe away all negative energy.
When you are completely relaxed stand up and move quietly to the
east quarter of your circle or room.

Light the east candle and say:
> *May the element of air bless this space with light, love and
> air and accept my gratitude for those gifts that I have been
> given.*

Light the south candle and say:
> *May the element of fire bless this space with light, love and
> fire and accept my gratitude for those gifts that I have
> been given.*

Light the west candle and say:
> *May the element of water bless this space with light, love
> and water and accept my gratitude for those gifts that I
> have been given.*

Light the north candle and say:
> *May the element of earth bless this space with light, love
> and earth and accept my gratitude for those gifts that I
> have been given.*

Move quietly back to your workspace and kneel in front of your table.
Light your white altar candle and meditate quietly on the Goddess Rangda.
In your mind give thanks for the gifts that you are showing gratitude for.
    See the abundance that you have been blessed with and say a prayer
in your own words to the Guardian Angel Gabriel.

Light your silver candle and, standing in front of your altar, raise your hands high above your head and say these words:

> I thank the Goddess for her blessings.
> I thank the Goddess for her gifts.
> For bringing me my heart's desire
> By the power of sacred fire.
> And it harm none so be it.

Spend some quiet time in your circle and allow your altar candle to burn through to the end but if you must put it out do so with a candle snuff or pinch the wick between dampened fingertips.

When you are finished working move quietly to the left of your circle.

Extinguish the east candle and say:
> I thank the element of air for blessing me with the gifts I have been given.

Extinguish the south candle and say:
> I thank the element of fire for blessing me with the gifts I have been given.

Extinguish the west candle and say:
> I thank the element of water for blessing me with the gifts I have been given.

Extinguish the north candle and say:
> I thank the element of earth for blessing me with the gifts I have been given.

Close your circle by saying:
> May the four powers give back to the universe any powers and energies that have not been used.
> The work is now done and the circle is closed.
> So mote it be.

Gratitude spell 2

10 mls of almond oil
Bergamot pure essential oil
A bottle for your oil mixture
A small face cloth or some tissues (to clean your hands after working with the oil)

Any item that you are grateful for or something that represents
    gratitude (For instance if you are showing gratitude for the
    birth of a child or the recovery of someone who has been ill
    you could use a photograph of that person)
Your favourite crystal or a piece of moonstone
Any silver items
One tall silver taper candle and holder
One tall white taper candle and holder
One small pointed knife
An ashtray or a small fireproof dish for spent matches or
    any paper that you may light during your spell and some
    matches or a lighter

Prepare a blend of oils using 10 mls of almond oil and add three drops
of bergamot pure essential oil. Hold the bottle of oil in your hands in
the prayer position and rub the bottle vigorously between the palms
of your hands and, as you do so, visualise the oil being empowered
with gratitude. When you feel as though the oil has been charged,
place it on your altar or work surface ready for use along with the
other ingredients.

Place four small candles at the east, south, west and north in that
order. Sit or kneel comfortably in front of your table. Close your eyes
and as you breathe in, picture positive, white, light energy filling
your body.

When you are completely relaxed stand up and move quietly to the
east quarter of your room.

Light the east candle and say:
    May the element of air bless this space with light, love and
    air and accept my gratitude for those gifts that I have been
    given.

Light the south candle and say:
    May the element of fire bless this space with light, love and
    fire and accept my gratitude for those gifts that I have
    been given.

Light the west candle and say:
    May the element of water bless this space with light, love
    and water and accept my gratitude for those gifts that I
    have been given.

Light the north candle and say:
    May the element of earth bless this space with light, love
    and earth and accept my gratitude for those gifts that I
    have been given.

Move quietly back to your workspace and kneel in front of your table. Light your white altar candle and meditate quietly on those aspects that you are grateful for. Take your silver spell candle and the small pointed knife and inscribe the number three and the rune symbol Ken at the top of the candle.

Place the candle back in the holder and, taking the bottle of empowered oil, place some in the palms of your hands. Rub your hands together and visualise that you are charging the energy in the oil and in your hands. Your hands will begin to feel very warm. Take the spell candle and spread the oil from middle to top and middle to bottom of the candle until the candle is completely covered in oil. Visualise that you are empowering the candle with your gratitude. Rub your hands vigorously together with the candle still held between the palms of your hands. After a few minutes, place your candle back in its holder and light the flame and say these words:

> The Goddess to me has been kind,
> And brought to me some peace of mind.
> I now give thanks for those gifts given,
> And bless each day the sun arisen.
> So mote it be.

Allow your candle to burn for as long as possible but if you must put it out do not blow it out otherwise you will reverse or negate your spell. You can use a candle snuff or pinch the flame between your thumb and finger. You may light your candle again but, each time you do so, visualise your wish as though it has already begun to happen. When you are finished working clean your hands on the cloth and move quietly to the left of your room.

Extinguish the east candle and say:
> I thank the element of air for blessing me with the gifts I have been given.

Extinguish the south candle and say:
> I thank the element of fire for blessing me with the gifts I have been given.

Extinguish the west candle and say:
> I thank the element of water for blessing me with the gifts I have been given.

Extinguish the north candle and say:
  I thank the element of earth for blessing me with the gifts
  I have been given.

Close your circle by saying:
  May the four powers give back to the universe any powers
  and energies that have not been used.
  The work is now done and the circle is closed.
  So mote it be.

4 Communication

Day of the week: The best day of the week is Wednesday
Time of day: The best time of day is 5am. Also noon, 7pm or at any time in the evening when the moon is waxing or full but not when it is waning
Goddess: Shakti
Planet: Mercury
Guardian Angel: Raphael
Star sign: Scorpio
Metal: Silver
Colour: Green
Rune: Ansur (also known as Ansuz)
Symbol: Writing materials
Number: Six
Crystal: Malachite
Flower: White lotus or chrysanthemum
Essential oil: Geranium
Herb: Parsley
Tree: Rowan

Mercury

Scorpio

Ansur

Communication spell 1

Prepare yourself and decorate your work surface or altar space with all your chosen ingredients such as:

White flowers
One white and one green taper candle and candle holders
A silver pen or a pen with silver ink and a piece of writing paper
A piece of malachite
An ashtray or a small fireproof dish for spent matches or
    any paper that you may light during your spell and some
    matches or a lighter

When you are ready and everything is in place, stand at the edge of your circle. Close your eyes and breathe in, visualising light energy filling your body. Breathe out and breathe away all negative energy. When you are completely relaxed stand up and move quietly to the east quarter of your circle or room.

Light the east candle and say:
    May the element of air bless this space with light, love and air and grant me the ability to listen with understanding and speak with wisdom.

Light the south candle and say:
    May the element of fire bless this space with light, love and fire and grant me the ability to listen with understanding and speak with wisdom.

Light the west candle and say:
    May the element of water bless this space with light, love and water and grant me the ability to listen with understanding and speak with wisdom.

Light the north candle and say:
    May the element of earth bless this space with light, love and earth and grant me the ability to listen with understanding and speak with wisdom.

Move quietly back to your workspace and kneel in front of your table and light your white altar candle.

Using your pen and paper, write your favourite verse or prayer. Hold the malachite crystal in your left hand and meditate quietly on the God Amotken and the Goddess Shakti. In your mind ask for the blessings of communication so that you may listen with understanding and speak with wisdom. Ask the Guardian Angel Raphael to bless your mouth, ears, nose and throat. Light your green candle, and using this candle, set light to the paper on which you have written your prayer or verse. Allow the burning paper to burn to ash in the fireproof dish.

Stand in front of your altar, raise your hands high above your head and say these words:

> *Amotken, Shakti hear me pray,*
> *Listen to the words I say.*
> *May wisdom bless my tongue, my lips*
> *Your guidance at my fingertips.*
> *And it harm none so be it.*

Spend some quiet time in your circle and allow your candles to burn through to the end but if you must put them out do so with a candle snuff or pinch the wick between dampened fingertips. When you are finished working move quietly to the left of your circle.

Extinguish the east candle and say:
> *I thank the element of air for blessing me with the ability to listen with understanding and speak with wisdom.*

Extinguish the south candle and say:
> *I thank the element of fire for blessing me with the ability to listen with understanding and speak with wisdom.*

Extinguish the west candle and say:
> *I thank the element of water for blessing me with the ability to listen with understanding and speak with wisdom.*

Extinguish the north candle and say:
> *I thank the element of earth for blessing me with the ability to listen with understanding and speak with wisdom.*

Close your circle by saying:
> *May the four powers give back to the universe any powers and energies that have not been used.*
> *The work is now done and the circle is closed.*
> *So mote it be.*

Communication spell 2

10 mls almond oil
Geranium pure essential oil
A bottle for your oil mixture
A small face cloth or some tissues (to clean your hands after
    working with the oil)
A malachite crystal
Any silver items
Any items representing communication such as a telephone,
    pens, or paper
One tall green candle and one tall white candle and holders
One small pointed knife
An ashtray or a small fireproof dish for spent matches or
    any paper that you may light during your spell and some
    matches or a lighter.

Prepare a blend of oils using 10 mls of almond oil and add three drops
of geranium pure essential oil. Hold the bottle of oil in your hands in
the prayer position and rub the bottle vigorously between the palms of
your hands and, as you do so, visualise the oil being empowered with
gratitude. When you feel as though the oil has been charged place it on
your altar or work surface ready for use along with the other ingredients.

Place four small candles at the east, south, west and north in that
order. Sit or kneel comfortably in front of your table. Close your eyes
and as you breathe in, picture positive white light energy filling your
body. When you are completely relaxed stand up and move quietly to
the east quarter of your room.

Light the east candle and say:
    May the element of air bless this space with light, love and
    air and grant me the ability to listen with understanding
    and speak with wisdom.

Light the south candle and say:
    May the element of fire bless this space with light, love and
    fire and grant me the ability to listen with understanding
    and speak with wisdom.

Light the west candle and say:
    May the element of water bless this space with light, love and
    water and grant me the ability to listen with understanding
    and speak with wisdom.

Light the north candle and say:
>   *May the element of earth bless this space with light, love and*
>   *earth and grant me the ability to listen with understanding*
>   *and speak with wisdom.*

Move quietly back to your workspace and kneel in front of your table.
Light your white altar candle and meditate quietly on the qualities that
you wish to be blessed with. Take your green spell candle and the small
pointed knife and inscribe the number six and the rune symbol Ansur
at the top of the candle. Place the candle back in the holder and taking
the bottle of empowered oil place some in the palm of your hands. Rub
your hands together and visualise that you are charging the energy
in the oil and in your hands. Your hands will begin to feel very warm.
Take the spell candle again and spread the oil from middle to top and
middle to bottom of the candle until the candle is completely covered
in oil. Visualise that you are empowering the candle with communication. Rub your hands vigorously together with the candle still held
between the palms of your hands.

After a few minutes, place your candle back in its holder and light
the flame and say these words:

>   *Candle burning precious light,*
>   *Bring to me this very night*
>   *Messages from far and near.*
>   *Help me listen help me hear.*
>   *And it harm none so mote it be.*

Allow your candle to burn for as long as possible but if you must put it
out do not blow it out otherwise you will reverse or negate your spell.
You can use a candle snuff or pinch the flame between your thumb
and finger. You may light your candle again but each time you do so
visualise your wish as though it has already begun to happen. When
you are finished working, clean your hands on the cloth and move
quietly to the left of your room.

Extinguish the east candle and say:
>   *I thank the element of air for blessing me with the ability to*
>   *listen with understanding and speak with wisdom.*

Extinguish the south candle and say:
>   *I thank the element of fire for blessing me with the ability to*
>   *listen with understanding and speak with wisdom.*

Extinguish the west candle and say:
*I thank the element of water for blessing me with the ability
to listen with understanding and speak with wisdom.*

Extinguish the north candle and say:
*I thank the element of earth for blessing me with the ability
to listen with understanding and speak with wisdom.*

Close your circle by saying:
*May the four powers give back to the universe any powers
and energies that have not been used.
The work is now done and the circle is closed.
So mote it be.*

5 Courage

Day of the week: The best day of the week is Tuesday
Time of Day: The best time of day is 5am. Also noon, 7pm or at any time in the evening when the moon is waxing or full but not when it is waning.
God: Bes
Goddess: Lillith
Planet: Mars
Guardian Angel: Samael
Star Sign: Aries
Metal: Iron
Colour: Red
Rune: Tir (also known as Tiwaz, or Tiewaz)
Symbol: Sword
Number: Four
Crystal: Jade, bloodstone or malachite
Flower: Honeysuckle
Essential oil: Lavender
Herb: Pepper
Tree: Holly

Mars

Aries

Tir

Courage spell 1

Prepare yourself and decorate your work surface or altar space with all your chosen ingredients such as:

A red cloth
Some honeysuckle or holly
Some jade, bloodstone or malachite crystals
One red taper candle and holder
One white taper candle and holder
An oil burner to which you have added some lavender essential
    oil and a pinch of black pepper

When you are ready and everything is in place, stand at the edge of your circle. Close your eyes and breathe in, visualising light energy filling your body. Breathe out and breathe away all negative energy. When you are completely relaxed, stand up and move quietly to the east quarter of your circle or room.

Light the east candle and say:
    May the element of air bless this space with light, love and
    air and grant me courage.

Light the south candle and say:
    May the element of fire bless this space with light, love and
    fire and grant me courage.

Light the west candle and say:
    May the element of water bless this space with light, love
    and Water and grant me courage.

Light the north candle and say:
    May the element of earth bless this space with light, love
    and earth and grant me courage.

Move quietly back to your workspace and kneel in front of your table. Light your white altar candle and meditate quietly on the God Bes and the Goddess Lillith asking for courage for the challenge, which lies ahead.

See yourself in triumph as though the victory is already yours and say a prayer in your own words to the Guardian Angel Samael.

Light your red candle and standing in front of your altar, raise your hands high above your head and say these words:

> *Courage and strength I possess*
> *Given to me by Lillith and Bes.*
> *Samael he blesses me,*
> *So that everyone can see.*
> *And it harm none so be it.*

Spend some quiet time in your circle and allow your candles to burn through to the end. If you must put your candles out use a candle snuff or pinch the wick between a dampened finger and thumb. When you are finished working move quietly to the left of your circle.

Extinguish the east candle and say:
> *I thank the element of air for blessing me with courage.*

Extinguish the south candle and say:
> *I thank the element of fire for blessing me with courage.*

Extinguish the west candle and say:
> *I thank the element of water for blessing me with courage.*

Extinguish the north candle and say:
> *I thank the element of earth for blessing me with courage.*

Close your circle by saying:
> *May the four powers give back to the universe any powers*
> *and energies that have not been used.*
> *The work is now done and the circle is closed.*
> *So mote it be.*

Courage spell 2

10 mls almond oil
Lavender pure essential oil
A bottle for your oil mixture
A small face cloth or some tissues (to clean your hands after
    working with the oil)
An item that represents victory, for instance, a medal or trophy
    would be ideal
Something made of iron or steel
A sword or dagger
A piece of jade, bloodstone or malachite
One tall red taper candle and holder
One tall white taper candle and holder
One small pointed knife

Prepare a blend of oils using 10 mls of almond oil and add three drops of lavender pure essential oil. Hold the bottle of oil in your hands in the prayer position and rub the bottle vigorously between the palms of your hands and as you do so visualise the oil being empowered with courage. When you feel as though the oil has been charged, place it on your altar or work surface ready for use along with the other ingredients.

Place four small candles at the east, south, west and north in that order. Sit or kneel comfortably in front of your table.

Close your eyes and, as you breathe in, picture positive, white light energy filling your body. When you are completely relaxed stand up and move quietly to the east quarter of your room.

Light the east candle and say:

> May the element of air bless this space with light, love and air and grant me courage.

Light the south candle and say:

> May the element of fire bless this space with light, love and fire and grant me courage.

Light the west candle and say:

> May the element of water bless this space with light, love and water and grant me courage.

Light the north candle and say:

> May the element of earth bless this space with light, love and earth and grant me courage.

Move quietly back to your workspace and kneel in front of your table. Light your white altar candle and meditate quietly on the challenge that requires courage and victory. Take your red spell candle and the small pointed knife and inscribe the number eight and the rune symbol Tir at the top of the candle. Place the candle back in the holder and, taking the bottle of empowered oil, place some in the palm of your hands. Rub your hands together and visualise that you are charging the energy in the oil and in your hands. Your hands will begin to feel very warm. Take the spell candle and spread the oil from middle to top and middle to bottom of the candle until the candle is completely covered in oil.

Visualise that you are empowering the candle with your courage and victory. Rub your hands vigorously together with the candle still held between the palms of your hands.

After a few minutes, place your candle back in its holder and light the flame and say these words:

> Burning flame that burns so true
> Bring to me the courage to
> Make me strong both day and night
> To meet this challenge with my might.
> Victory it shall be mine.
> Blessed be the powers that shine.
> And it harm none so mote it be.

Allow your candle to burn for as long as possible, but if you must put it out do not blow it out otherwise you will reverse or negate your spell. You can use a candle snuff or pinch the flame between your thumb and finger. You may light your candle again but, each time you do so, visualise your wish as though it has already begun to happen. When you are finished working, clean your hands on the cloth and move quietly to the left of your room.

Extinguish the east candle and say:
> I thank the element of air for blessing me with courage.

Extinguish the south candle and say:
> I thank the element of fire for blessing me with courage.

Extinguish the west candle and say:
> I thank the element of water for blessing me with courage.

Extinguish the north candle and say:
> I thank the element of earth for blessing me with courage.

Close your circle by saying:
> May the four powers give back to the universe any powers
> and energies that have not been used.
> The work is now done and the circle is closed.
> So mote it be.

6 Forgiveness

Day of the week: The best day of the week is Wednesday
Time of day: The best time of day is 5am. Also noon, 7pm or at any time in the evening when the moon is waxing or full but not when it is waning
God: Zeus
Goddess: Hera
Planet: Neptune
Guardian Angel: Sabbathi
Star sign: Pisces
Metal: Platinum
Colour: Violet
Rune Symbol: Eolh (also known as Elhaz or Algiz)
Number: Six
Crystal: Apache teardrop
Flower: Daffodil
Essential oil: Cedarwood
Herb: Angelica
Tree: Ash

Neptune

Pisces

Eolh

Forgiveness spell 1

Prepare yourself and decorate your work surface or altar space with all your chosen ingredients such as:

A purple- or violet-coloured cloth
A bowl of daffodils
A piece of writing paper
A pen
Any silver or platinum items
One violet, purple or silver taper candle and holder
One white taper candle and holder
A piece of angelica
A piece of apache teardrop
A small twig of an ash tree

When you are ready and everything is in place, stand at the edge of your circle. Close your eyes and breathe in, visualising light energy filling your body. Breathe out and breathe away all negative energy. When you are completely relaxed stand up and move quietly to the east quarter of your circle or room.

Light the east candle and say:
   May the element of air bless this space with light, love and air and grant me the ability to forgive (or grant me forgiveness).

Light the south candle and say:
   May the element of fire bless this space with light, love and fire and grant me the ability to forgive (or grant me forgiveness).

Light the west candle and say:
   May the element of water bless this space with light, love and water and grant me the ability to forgive (or grant me forgiveness).

Light the north candle and say:
   May the element of earth bless this space with light, love and earth and grant me the ability to forgive (or grant me forgiveness).

Move quietly back to your workspace and kneel in front of your table. Light your white altar candle and meditate quietly on the God

Zeus and or the Goddess Hera. In your mind ask that you be granted forgiveness or ask that you have the ability to forgive. Write down a brief outline of the situation that requires forgiveness. This could be something that you want to be forgiven for or it could be something that you want to forgive another for.

Say a prayer in your own words to the Guardian Angel Sabbathi.

Light your violet, purple or silver taper candle and taking your paper light it from the coloured candle. Let it burn through in the fireproof dish. Stand in front of your altar.

Raise your hands high above your head and say these words:

> Zeus and Hera hear me pray.
> Hurts to me are now forgiven
> 'Sorry', be the word I say
> Love restored my joy has risen
> And it harm none so be it.

Spend some quiet time in your circle and allow your altar candle to burn through to the end but if you must put it out do so with a candle snuff or pinch the wick between dampened fingertips. When you are finished working move quietly to the left of your circle.

Extinguish the east candle and say:
> I thank the element of air for blessing me with the ability to forgive (or granting me forgiveness).

Extinguish the south candle and say:
> I thank the element of fire for blessing me with the ability to forgive (or granting me forgiveness).

Extinguish the west candle and say:
> I thank the element of water for blessing me with the ability to forgive (or granting me forgiveness).

Extinguish the north candle and say:
> I thank the element of earth for blessing me with the ability to forgive (or granting me forgiveness).

Close your circle by saying:
> May the four powers give back to the universe any powers and energies that have not been used.
> The work is now done and the circle is closed.
> So mote it be.

Forgiveness spell 2

10 mls almond oil
Cedarwood pure essential oil
A bottle for your oil mixture
A small face cloth or some tissues (to clean your hands after
    working with the oil)
A piece of apache teardrop
A vase of violets or daffodils or any other yellow or violet col-
    oured flower
One tall violet or purple taper candle and holder
One small pointed knife
An ashtray or a small fireproof dish for spent matches or
    any paper that you may light during your spell and some
    matches or a lighter.

Prepare a blend of oils using 10 mls of almond oil and add three drops of cedarwood pure essential oil. Hold the bottle of oil in your hands in the prayer position and rub the bottle vigorously between the palms of your hands and, as you do so, visualise the oil being empowered with gratitude. When you feel as though the oil has been charged place it on your altar or work surface ready for use along with the other ingredients.

Place four small candles at the east, south, west and north in that order.

Sit or kneel comfortably in front of your table. Close your eyes and, as you breathe in, picture positive, white light energy filling your body. When you are completely relaxed stand up and move quietly to the east quarter of your room.

Light the east candle and say:
    *May the element of air bless this space with light, love and air
    and grant me the ability to forgive (or grant me forgiveness).*

Light the south candle and say:
    *May the element of fire bless this space with light, love
    and fire and grant me the ability to forgive (or grant me
    forgiveness).*

Light the west candle and say:
    *May the element of water bless this space with light, love
    and water and grant me the ability to forgive (or grant me
    forgiveness).*

Light the north candle and say:
   *May the element of earth bless this space with light, love
   and earth and grant me the ability to forgive (or grant me
   forgiveness).*

Move quietly back to your workspace and kneel in front of your table.
Light your white altar candle and meditate quietly on being forgiven
or giving forgiveness.

Take your violet spell candle and the small pointed knife and
inscribe the number six and the rune symbol Eolh at the top of the
candle. Place the candle back in the holder and, taking the bottle of
empowered oil, place some in the palm of your hands. Rub your hands
together and visualise that you are charging the energy in the oil and
in your hands. Your hands will begin to feel very warm. Take the spell
candle and spread the oil from middle to top and middle to bottom
of the candle until the candle is completely covered in oil. Visualise
that you are empowering the spell candle with forgiveness. Rub your
hands vigorously together with the candle still held between the palms
of your hands.

After a few minutes, place your candle back in its holder and light
the flame and say these words:

> *Life's too short to hold a grudge,*
> *Deeds forgotten do not judge,*
> *Forgiveness now I pray this day,*
> *Let love return and sorrow away.*
> *And it harm none so mote it be.*

Allow your candle to burn for as long as possible but, if you must put it
out, do not blow it out otherwise you will reverse or negate your spell.
You can use a candle snuff or pinch the flame between your thumb
and finger. You may light your candle again but each time you do so
visualise your wish as though it has already begun to happen. When
you are finished working clean your hands on the cloth and move
quietly to the left of your room.

Extinguish the east candle and say:
   *I thank the element of air for blessing me with the ability to
   forgive (or for granting me forgiveness).*

Extinguish the south candle and say:
   *I thank the element of fire for blessing me with the ability to
   forgive (or for granting me forgiveness).*

Extinguish the west candle and say:
> I thank the element of water for blessing me with the ability
> to forgive (or for granting me forgiveness).

Extinguish the north candle and say:
> I thank the element of earth for blessing me with the ability
> to forgive (or for granting me forgiveness).

Close your circle by saying:
> May the four powers give back to the universe any powers
> and energies that have not been used.
> The work is now done and the circle is closed.
> So mote it be.

7 Inspiration

Day of the week: The best day of the week is Saturday
Time of day: The best time of day is 5am. Also noon, 7pm or at any time in the evening when the moon is waxing or full but not when it is waning
God: Telesphoros
Goddess: Ostara
Planet: Uranus
Guardian Angel: Arvath
Star sign: Aquarius
Metal: Aluminium
Colour: Indigo
Rune: Ansur (also known as Ansuz)
Symbol: Key
Number: One
Crystal: Amethyst
Flower: Anemones
Essential oil: Peppermint
Herb: Sage
Tree: Hazel

Uranus

Aquarius

Ansur

Inspiration spell 1

Prepare yourself and decorate your work surface or altar space with all your chosen ingredients such as:

Keys
Any book that inspires you
Any aluminium items (for instance you could cover your favour-
    ite vase or candle holder with aluminium foil)
One indigo taper candle and holder
One white taper candle and holder
A vase of anemones
A sprig or pinch of sage
A twig from a hazel tree
A piece of amethyst crystal
An ashtray or a small fireproof dish for spent matches or
    any paper that you may light during your spell and some
    matches or a lighter

When you are ready and everything is in place, stand at the edge of your circle. Close your eyes and breathe in, visualising light energy filling your body. Breathe out and breathe away all negative energy. When you are completely relaxed stand up and move quietly to the east quarter of your circle or room.

Light the east candle and say:
    May the element of air bless this space with light, love and
    air and grant me inspiration.

Light the south candle and say:
    May the element of fire bless this space with light, love and
    fire and grant me inspiration.

Light the west candle and say:
    May the element of water bless this space with light, love
    and water and grant me inspiration.

Light the north candle and say:
    May the element of earth bless this space with light, love
    and earth and grant me inspiration.

Move quietly back to your workspace and kneel in front of your table. Light your white altar candle and holding your crystal in your left hand meditate quietly on the God Telesphoros and the Goddess Ostara. In your mind and heart, begin to feel excitement and motivation build. Say a prayer in your own words to the Guardian Angel Arvath.

Light your indigo candle, stand in front of your altar, raise your hands high above your head and say these words:

> May the light of inspiration
> Motivate and guide my way.
> To Telesphoros and Ostara
> These sacred words I pray.
> And it harm none so be it.

Spend some quiet time in your circle and allow your altar candle to burn through to the end but if you must put it out do so with a candle snuff or pinch the wick between dampened fingertips. When you are finished working move quietly to the left of your circle.

Extinguish the east candle and say:
> I thank the element of air for blessing me with inspiration.

Extinguish the south candle and say:
> I thank the element of fire for blessing me with inspiration.

Extinguish the west candle and say:
> I thank the element of water for blessing me with inspiration.

Extinguish the north candle and say:
> I thank the element of earth for blessing me with inspiration.

Close your circle by saying:
> May the four powers give back to the universe any powers
> and energies that have not been used.
> The work is now done and the circle is closed.
> So mote it be.

Place your crystal under your pillow and keep it there for the next seven nights. During the daytime when you are working hold your crystal in your left hand from time to time allowing inspiration to grow within you.

Inspiration spell 2

10 mls almond oil
Peppermint pure essential oil
A bottle for the oil mixture
A small face cloth or some tissues (to clean your hands after
    working with the oil)
A set of keys and a dictionary or thesaurus
An amethyst crystal
An oil burner to which you have added some water some sage
    and one drop of lemon pure essential oils
One tall indigo taper candle and holder
One tall white taper candle and holder
One small pointed knife

Prepare a blend of oils using 10 mls of almond oil and add three drops
of peppermint pure essential oil. Hold the bottle of oil in your hands in
the prayer position and rub the bottle vigorously between the palms
of your hands and as you do so visualise the oil being empowered
with gratitude. When you feel as though the oil has been charged,
place it on your altar or work surface ready for use along with the
other ingredients.

Place four small candles at the east, south, west and north in that order.

Sit or kneel comfortably in front of your table. Close your eyes and
as you breathe in, picture positive, white light energy filling your body.
When you are completely relaxed stand up and move quietly to the
east quarter of your room.

Light the east candle and say:
   May the element of air bless this space with light, love and
   air and grant me inspiration.

Light the south candle and say:
   May the element of fire bless this space with light, love and
   fire and grant me inspiration.

Light the west candle and say:
   May the element of water bless this space with light, love
   and water and grant me inspiration.

Light the north candle and say:
   May the element of earth bless this space with light, love
   and earth and grant me inspiration.

Move quietly back to your workspace and kneel in front of your table and light your white altar candle.

Meditate quietly on the area of your life that requires inspiration. Take your indigo spell candle and the small pointed knife and inscribe the number one and the rune symbol Ansur at the top of the candle. Place the candle back in the holder and, taking the bottle of empowered oil, place some in the palm of your hands. Rub your hands together and visualise that you are charging the energy in the oil and in your hands. Your hands will begin to feel very warm. Take the spell candle and spread the oil from middle to top and middle to bottom of the candle until the candle is completely covered in oil. Visualise that you are empowering the candle with your inspiration. Rub your hands vigorously together with the candle still held between the palms of your hands.

After a few minutes, place your candle back in its holder and light the flame and say these words:

> Angel Arvath, hear my plea,
> Inspiration send to me,
> Make ideas flow thick and fast,
> Projects planned to thrive and last.
> And it harm none so mote it be.

Allow your candle to burn for as long as possible but, if you must put it out, do not blow it out otherwise you will reverse or negate your spell. You can use a candle snuff or pinch the flame between your thumb and finger. You may light your candle again but each time you do so visualise your wish as though it has already begun to happen. When you are finished working clean your hands on the cloth and move quietly to the left of your room.

Extinguish the east candle and say:
> I thank the element of air for blessing me with inspiration.

Extinguish the south candle and say:
> I thank the element of fire for blessing me with inspiration.

Extinguish the west candle and say:
> I thank the element of water for blessing me with inspiration.

Extinguish the north candle and say:
> I thank the element of earth for blessing me with inspiration.

Close your circle by saying:
> May the four powers give back to the universe any powers
> and energies that have not been used.
> The work is now done and the circle is closed.
> So mote it be.

8 Peace

Day of the week: The best day of the week is Friday
Time of day: The best time of day is 5am. Also noon, 7pm or at any time in the evening when the moon is waxing or full but not when it is waning
God: Wakantanka
Goddess: Pax
Planet: Venus
Guardian Angel: Arnad
Star sign: Taurus
Metal: Copper or rose gold
Colour: White
Rune: Othel (also known as Othala)
Symbol: Cone shaped items
Number: Two
Crystal: Rhodochrosite
Flower: White lily
Essential oil: Marjoram
Herb: Chamomile
Tree: Olive

Venus

Taurus

Othel

Peace spell 1

Prepare yourself and decorate your work surface or altar space with all your chosen ingredients such as:

Two white taper candles and holders
Items made of copper or rose gold
A vase of lilies or chamomile
A piece of rhodochrosite crystal
Shells or funnel-shaped items, which could possibly be made
     from paper
Photographs or pictures of doves
An ashtray or a small fireproof dish for spent matches or
     any paper that you may light during your spell and some
     matches or a lighter

When you are ready and everything is in place, stand at the edge of your circle. Close your eyes and breathe in, visualising light energy filling your body. Breathe out and breathe away all negative energy. When you are completely relaxed, stand up and move quietly to the east quarter of your circle or room.

Light the east candle and say:
     *May the element of air bless this space with light, love and
     air and grant me peace.*

Light the south candle and say:
     *May the element of fire bless this space with light, love and
     fire and grant me peace.*

Light the west candle and say:
     *May the element of water bless this space with light, love
     and water and grant me peace.*

Light the north candle and say:
     *May the element of earth bless this space with light, love
     and earth and grant me peace.*

Move quietly back to your workspace and kneel in front of your table. Light your white altar candle and, holding your crystal in your left hand, meditate quietly on the God Wakantanka and the Goddess Pax. In your mind and heart begin to feel a sense of peace and harmony filling your body and spirit. Say a prayer in your own words to the Guardian Angel Arnad.

Light your second candle, stand in front of your altar, raise your hands high above your head and say these words:

> Let peace be felt upon the land
> No weapons lifted by any hand
> Let us prosper as animals graze
> And Pax be with us to hear our praise
> And it harm none so be it.

When you have finished, put one silver coin into one of the shells. If it is possible, let the large white candle burn until it is finished.

Extinguish the east candle and say:
> I thank the element of air for blessing me with peace.

Extinguish the south candle and say:
> I thank the element of fire for blessing me with peace.

Extinguish the west candle and say:
> I thank the element of water for blessing me with peace.

Extinguish the north candle and say:
> I thank the element of earth for blessing me with peace.

Close your circle by saying:
> May the four powers give back to the universe any powers and energies that have not been used.
> The work is now done and the circle is closed.
> So mote it be

Each day, for thirty days, add one silver coin. This spell will work best if it is begun on the first day of the new moon. At the end of the thirty days give the coins you have collected to a charity or to a worthwhile cause.

Peace spell 2

10 mls almond oil
Marjoram pure essential oil
A bottle for your oil mixture
A small face cloth or some tissues (to clean your hands after working with the oil)
An item that represents peace to you
A rhodochrosite crystal

Two tall, white taper candles and holders
One small pointed knife

Prepare a blend of oils using 10 mls of almond oil and add three drops of marjoram essential oil. Hold the bottle of oil in your hands in the prayer position and rub the bottle vigorously between the palms of your hands and as you do so visualise the oil being empowered with gratitude. When you feel as though the oil has been charged place it on your altar or work surface ready for use along with the other ingredients.

Place four small candles at the east, south, west and north in that order. Sit or kneel comfortably in front of your table. Close your eyes and, as you breathe in, picture positive, white light energy filling your body.

When you are completely relaxed stand up and move quietly to the east quarter of your room.

Light the east candle and say:
   May the element of air bless this space with light, love and air and grant me peace.

Light the south candle and say:
   May the element of fire bless this space with light, love and fire and grant me peace.

Light the west candle and say:
   May the element of water bless this space with light, love and water and grant me peace.

Light the north candle and say:
   May the element of earth bless this space with light, love and earth and grant me peace.

Move quietly back to your workspace and kneel in front of your table. Light your white altar candle and meditate quietly on Wakantanka, the supreme being. Take your second white candle and the small pointed knife and inscribe the number two and the rune symbol Othel at the top of the candle. Place the candle back in the holder and taking the bottle of empowered oil place some in the palm of your hands. Rub your hands together and visualise that you are charging the energy in the oil and in your hands. Your hands will begin to feel very warm. Take the spell candle and spread the oil from middle to top and middle to bottom of the candle until the candle is completely covered in oil.

Visualise that you are empowering the candle with peace. Rub your hands vigorously together with the candle still held between the palms of your hands. After a few minutes, place your candle back in its holder and light the flame and say these words.

> Wakantanka hear me pray,
> Let peace be with us on this day.
> No more trouble, no more strife,
> Peace and harmony fill my life.
> And it harm none so mote it be.

Allow your candle to burn for as long as possible but, if you must put it out, do not blow it out otherwise you will reverse or negate your spell. You can use a candle snuff or pinch the flame between your thumb and finger. You may light your candle again but, each time you do so, visualise your wish as though it has already begun to happen. When you are finished working, clean your hands on the cloth and move quietly to the left of your room.

Extinguish the east candle and say:
   I thank the element of air for blessing me with peace.

Extinguish the south candle and say:
   I thank the element of fire for blessing me with peace.

Extinguish the west candle and say:
   I thank the element of water for blessing me with peace.

Extinguish the north candle and say:
   I thank the element of earth for blessing me with peace.

Close your circle by saying:
   May the four powers give back to the universe any powers
   and energies that have not been used.
   The work is now done and the circle is closed.
   So mote it be.

9 Health

Day of the week: The best day of the week is Sunday
Time of day: The best time of day is 5am. Also noon, 7pm or at any time in the evening when the moon is waxing or full but not when it is waning
Goddess: Brigit
Planet: Neptune
Guardian Angel: Germaine
Star sign: Pisces
Metal: Gold
Colour: Green yellow or violet
Rune: Beork
Symbol: Fish
Number: Three
Crystal: Clear quartz
Flower: Marigold, daffodil or sunflower
Essential oil: Sandalwood
Herb: Lavender
Tree: Ash

Neptune

Pisces

Beork

Health spell 1

Prepare yourself and decorate your work surface or altar space with all your chosen ingredients such as:

A green, yellow or violet cloth
Any items made of gold
One green and one white taper candle and holders
A spray of marigolds, daffodils or sunflowers
A piece of clear quartz crystal

When you are ready and everything is in place, stand at the edge of your circle. Close your eyes and breathe in, visualising light energy filling your body. Breathe out and breathe away all negative energy. When you are completely relaxed, stand up and move quietly to the east quarter of your circle or room.

Light the east candle and say:
　　May the element of air bless this space with light, love and air and grant good health.

Light the south candle and say:
　　May the element of fire bless this space with light, love and fire and grant me good health.

Light the west candle and say:
　　May the element of water bless this space with light, love and water and grant me good health.

Light the north candle and say:
　　May the element of earth bless this space with light, love and earth and grant me good health.

Move quietly back to your workspace and kneel in front of your table. Light your white altar candle and meditate quietly on the Goddess Brigit. In your mind, visualise yourself or the person who you wish to be well in good health.

　　Say a prayer in your own words to the Guardian Angel Germaine.

　　Light your green candle and as the flame grows in strength visualise health improving.

　　Stand in front of your altar, raise your hands high above your head and say these words:

Flesh be healthy, spirit strong,
Dancing feet and joyful song,
Health restored, revitalised,
(Name) recovered before my eyes.
And it harm none so be it.

Spend some quiet time in your circle and allow your altar candle to burn through to the end but if you must put it out do so with a candle snuff or pinch the wick between dampened fingertips.

When you are finished working move quietly to the left of your circle.

Extinguish the east candle and say:
I thank the element of air for blessing me with good health.

Extinguish the south candle and say:
I thank the element of fire for blessing me with good health.

Extinguish the west candle and say:
I thank the element of water for blessing me with good health.

Extinguish the north candle and say:
I thank the element of earth for blessing me with good health.

Close your circle by saying:
May the four powers give back to the universe any powers and energies that have not been used.
The work is now done and the circle is closed.
So mote it be.

Health spell 2

10 mls almond oil
Sandalwood pure essential oil
A bottle for your oil mixture
A small face cloth or some tissues (to clean your hands after working with the oil)
A goldfish bowl and goldfish
A clear quartz crystal
A sprig of lavender or a pinch of dried lavender added to a burner
One tall green, yellow or violet taper candle
One white candle
Candle holders
One small pointed knife

Prepare a blend of oils using 10 mls of almond oil and add the three drops of sandalwood essential oil. Hold the bottle of oil in your hands in the prayer position and rub the bottle vigorously between the palms of your hands and as you do so visualise the oil being empowered with gratitude.

When you feel as though the oil has been charged place it on your altar or work surface ready for use along with the other ingredients.

Place four small candles at the east, south, west and north in that order. Sit or kneel comfortably in front of your table. Close your eyes and as you breathe in, picture positive, white light energy filling your body.

When you are completely relaxed stand up and move quietly to the east quarter of your room.

Light the east candle and say:
   May the element of air bless this space with light, love and air and grant good health.

Light the south candle and say:
   May the element of fire bless this space with light, love and fire and grant me good health.

Light the west candle and say:
   May the element of water bless this space with light, love and water and grant me good health.

Light the north candle and say:
   May the element of earth bless this space with light, love and earth and grant me good health.

Move quietly back to your workspace and kneel in front of your table. Light your white altar candle and meditate quietly on all the things that would be possible with good health.

Take your coloured spell candle and the small pointed knife and inscribe the number three and the rune symbol Beork at the top of the candle. Place the candle back in the holder and taking the bottle of empowered oil place some in the palm of your hands. Rub your hands together and visualise that you are charging the energy in the oil and in your hands. Your hands will begin to feel very warm. Take the spell candle and spread the oil from middle to top and middle to bottom of the candle until the candle is completely covered in oil.

Visualise that you are empowering the candle with good health. Rub your hands vigorously together with the candle still held between the palms of your hands. After a few minutes, place your candle back in its holder and light the flame and say these words:

> Swift and sure let healing come
> To us all the work is done
> Blessed be the guardians who
> Work to heal both me and you
> And it harm none so mote it be

Allow your candle to burn for as long as possible but, if you must put it out, do not blow it out otherwise you will reverse or negate your spell. You can use a candle snuff or pinch the flame between your thumb and finger. You may light your candle again but each time you do so visualise your wish as though it has already begun to happen. When you are finished working, clean your hands on the cloth and move quietly to the left of your room.

Extinguish the east candle and say:
> I thank the element of air for blessing me with good health.

Extinguish the south candle and say:
> I thank the element of fire for blessing me with good health.

Extinguish the west candle and say:
> I thank the element of water for blessing me with good health.

Extinguish the north candle and say:
> I thank the element of earth for blessing me with good health.

Close your circle by saying:
> May the four powers give back to the universe any powers and energies that have not been used.
> The work is now done and the circle is closed.
> So mote it be.

10 Love

Day of the week: The best day of the week is Friday
Time of day: The best time of day is 5am. Also noon, 7pm or at any time in the evening when the moon is waxing or full but not when it is waning
Goddess: Freya
Planets: Venus, Mars
Guardian Angel: Arnad
Star sign: Taurus
Metal: Copper or brass
Colour: Pink, red or orange
Rune: Ing (or Inguz), Mann
Symbol: Hearts
Number: Two
Crystal: Rose quartz, emerald or sapphire
Flower: Lavender, lilac, red, rose or jasmine
Essential oil: Rose Bulgar, rose Maroc, ylang ylang, geranium or jasmine
Herb: Rose
Tree: Apple

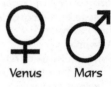

Venus   Mars

Taurus

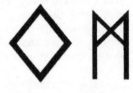

Ing   Mann

Love spell 1

Prepare yourself and decorate your work surface or altar space with all your chosen ingredients such as:

Hearts, rings and symbols of love and romance
Items made of copper or brass
A piece of rose quartz
Two red roses
An apple
Some pictures of happy couples holding hands or kissing (ideally, close family or friends whom you know have happy relationships)
One white and one pink taper candle and holders
An oil burner to which you have added essential oil of ylang ylang or patchouli
A small flowerpot filled with potting compost
A sharp knife
A small glass of water

When you are ready and everything is in place, stand at the edge of your circle. Close your eyes and breathe in, visualising light energy filling your body. Breathe out and breathe away all negative energy. When you are completely relaxed, stand up and move quietly to the east quarter of your circle or room.

Light the east candle and say:
    May the element of air bless this space with light, love and air and grant true love given and returned alike.

Light the south candle and say:
    May the element of fire bless this space with light, love and fire and grant true love given and returned alike.

Light the west candle and say:
    May the element of water bless this space with light, love and water and grant true love given and returned alike.

Light the north candle and say:
    May the element of earth bless this space with light, love and earth and grant true love given and returned alike.

Move quietly back to your workspace and kneel in front of your table.

Light your white altar candle and meditate quietly on the Goddess Venus. In your mind see yourself in a loving relationship. Say a prayer in your own words to the Guardian Angel Arnad. Light your pink candle and, standing in front of your altar, raise your hands high above your head and say these words.

> Venus shining in the night,
> Bless my heart with love and light.
> Loved in truth I wish to be,
> Listen to my prayer, my plea.
> May I love and be loved too,
> Blessed be the love that's true.
> And it harm none so be it.

Spend some quiet time in your circle and allow your pink candle to burn through to the end.

While your candle is burning, peel and core your apple, carefully removing the pips and place them in the small flowerpot. Pour some water over the pips that you have planted and say:

> As the seeds I have planted begin to grow,
> May the love that I have begin to show.

When you are finished move quietly to the left of your circle.

Extinguish the east candle and say:
   I thank the element of air for blessing me with a loving and happy relationship.

Extinguish the south candle and say:
   I thank the element of fire for blessing me with a loving and happy relationship.

Extinguish the west candle and say:
   I thank the element of water for blessing me with a loving and happy relationship.

Extinguish the north candle and say:
   I thank the element of earth for blessing me with a loving and happy relationship.

Close your circle by saying:
  May the four powers give back to the universe any powers
  and energies that have not been used.
  The work is now done and the circle is closed.
  So mote it be.

Set your planted seeds in an area where they will be blessed by light
and nourish them with water and love.

Love spell 2

A piece of rose quartz, jade, aventurine or moonstone.
A small dish of the herbs chamomile, sorrel or bay
A small posy of gardenias, tansies or roses
A small bottle of 'romance blend' oil: 10 mls of sunflower oil, one
  drop of rose absolute, Bulgar, Maroc or Egyptian. (These oils
  are expensive so you can substitute three drops of patchouli,
  jasmine, ylang ylang or geranium)
A small face cloth or some tissues
A small fireproof dish for matches or burning herbs or paper
Any items that you consider to be symbolic of love or romance
One white, and two pink, tall taper candles and holders
One small pointed knife
A small fireproof dish or an ashtray for spent matches or
  any paper that you may light during your spell and some
  matches or a lighter

Place four small candles at the east, south, west, and north in that
order.
    When everything is in place, sit or kneel comfortably in front of your
table. Close your eyes and as you breathe in, picture positive, white
light energy filling your body. As you breathe out, breathe away all
negative energy. After some minutes, you will feel all tension flowing
away from your mind and body. Allow pure light energy to flow into
and through your entire body filling your sacred space, filling your
room. When you are completely relaxed stand up and move quietly
to the east quarter of your room.

Light the east candle and say:
  May the element of air bless this space with light, love and
  air and grant me the love that I desire. As I give love so shall
  I receive love.

Light the south candle and say:
>   *May the element of fire bless this space with light, love and*
>   *fire and grant me the love that I desire. As I give love so*
>   *shall I receive love.*

Light the west candle and say:
>   *May the element of water bless this space with light, love*
>   *and water and grant me the love that I desire. As I give love*
>   *so shall I receive love.*

Light the north candle and say:
>   *May the element of earth bless this space with light, love*
>   *and earth and grant me the love that I desire. As I give love*
>   *so shall I receive love.*

Move quietly back to your workspace and kneel in front of your table. Light your white altar candle and meditate quietly on your hearts desire and see your wish come true.

Take one of your pink spell candles and the small pointed knife and inscribe the symbol for Venus at the top of the candle. Place the candle back in the holder and taking the bottle of empowered oil place some in the palm of your hands. Rub your hands together and visualise that you are charging the energy in the oil and in your hands. Your hands will begin to feel very warm. At this point take the first pink spell candle and spread the oil from middle to top and middle to bottom of the candle until the candle is completely covered in oil.

While you are doing this visualise that you are empowering the candle with your desire. Keep thinking about your heartfelt desire and whilst doing this rub your hands vigorously together with the candle still held between the palms of your hands. After a few minutes, place your candle back in its holder. Now take the second pink candle and the small knife and inscribe the symbol for Mars and the rune symbols Mann and Ing.

Anoint your candle as before and put it into the candle holder. Light both pink candles and say these words:

>   *Love to me I pray you bring*
>   *By the power of love so true.*
>   *Fill my heart so it may sing,*
>   *Rejoice and let me love anew.*
>   *And it harm none so be it.*

Allow your altar candle to burn for as long as possible but if you must put it out do not blow it. You may light your candle again but each time you do so visualise your wish as though it has already begun to happen. When you are finished working clean your hands on the cloth and move quietly to the left of your room.

Extinguish the east candle and say:
> I thank the element of air for blessing me with a loving and happy relationship.

Extinguish the south candle and say:
> I thank the element of fire for blessing me with a loving and happy relationship.

Extinguish the west candle and say:
> I thank the element of water for blessing me with a loving and happy relationship.

Extinguish the north candle and say:
> I thank the element of earth for blessing me with a loving and happy relationship.

Close your circle by saying
> May the four powers give back to the universe any powers and energies that have not been used.
> The work is now done and the circle is closed.
> So mote it be.

The following day, set two candles at opposite ends of your room and light them repeating the words:

> Love to me I pray you bring
> By the power of love so true.
> Fill my heart so it may sing,
> Rejoice and let me love anew.
> And it harm none so be it.

Do this every day for thirty days, moving the candles closer and closer together until they sit side by side. Let your candles burn for as long as possible or put them out with a candle snuff.

11 Career

Day of the week: The best day of the week is Sunday
Time of day: The best time of day is 5am. Also noon, 7pm or at any time in the evening when the moon is waxing or full but not when it is waning.
Goddess: Oshion
Planet: Sun
Guardian Angel: Michael
Star sign: Leo
Metal: Gold
Colour: Yellow or orange
Rune: Tir (also known as Tiwaz)
Symbol: Keys
Number: Five
Crystal: Citrine, tiger's eye, sunstone
Flower: Marigold
Essential oil: Bergamot
Herb: Chamomile
Tree: Hazel

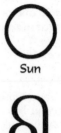

Sun

Leo

Tir

Career spell 1

Prepare yourself and decorate your work surface or altar space with all your chosen ingredients such as:

Any gold items
One gold and one white taper candle and holders
A vase of marigolds
Some keys
A piece of citrine, tiger's eye or sunstone

When you are ready and everything is in place, stand at the edge of your circle. Close your eyes and breathe in, visualising light energy filling your body. Breathe out and breathe away all negative energy. When you are completely relaxed stand up and move quietly to the east quarter of your circle or room.

Light the east candle and say:
    May the element of air bless this space with light, love and
    air and grant me the position I desire.

Light the south candle and say:
    May the element of fire bless this space with light, love and
    fire and grant me the position I desire.

Light the west candle and say:
    May the element of water bless this space with light, love
    and water and grant me the position I desire.

Light the north candle and say:
    May the element of Earth bless this space with light, love
    and Earth and grant me the position I desire.

Move quietly back to your workspace and kneel in front of your table. Light your white altar candle and meditate quietly on the Goddess Oshion.

See yourself in a worthwhile, well-paid position that you enjoy, and where you feel happy and content. Also visualise that you and your new work colleagues enjoy harmonious working relationships together and say a prayer in your own words to the Guardian Angel Michael.

Light your gold candle and, standing in front of your altar, raise your hands high above your head and say these words:

> Keys to open doors for me,
> Chances come to set me free,
> Ambitions reached and realised,
> Seen before my very eyes.
> And it harm none so be it.

Spend some quiet time in your circle and allow your candles to burn through to the end or put them out using a candle snuff. When you are finished working move quietly to the left of your circle.

Extinguish the east candle and say:
> I thank the element of air for blessing me with a new career.

Extinguish the south candle and say:
> I thank the element of fire for blessing me with a new career.

Extinguish the west candle and say:
> I thank the element of water for blessing me with a new career.

Extinguish the north candle and say:
> I thank the element of earth for blessing me with a new career.

Close your circle by saying:
> May the four powers give back to the universe any powers and energies that have not been used.
> The work is now done and the circle is closed.
> So mote it be.

Career spell 2

10 mls almond oil
3 drops of bergamot pure essential oil
A bottle for your oil mixture
A small face cloth or some tissues
A small fireproof dish for matches or burning herbs or paper
Your current CV or job applications
A piece of tiger's eye crystal
A sprig of hazel
One white and one orange, gold or yellow taper candle and
    holders
One small pointed knife

Prepare a blend of oils using 10 mls of almond oil and add three drops of bergamot pure essential oil. Hold the bottle of oil in your hands in the prayer position and rub the bottle vigorously between the palms of your hands and as you do so visualise the oil being empowered with gratitude. When you feel as though the oil has been charged place it on your altar or work surface ready for use along with the other items. Place four small candles at the east, south, west, and north in that order. Sit or kneel comfortably in front of your table. Close your eyes and as you breathe in, picture positive white light energy filling your body. When you are completely relaxed stand up and move quietly to the east quarter of your room.

Light the east candle and say:
> *May the element of air bless this space with light, love and air and grant me the position I desire.*

Light the south candle and say:
> *May the element of fire bless this space with light, love and fire and grant me the position I desire.*

Light the west candle and say:
> *May the element of water bless this space with light, love and water and grant me the position I desire.*

Light the north candle and say:
> *May the element of earth bless this space with light, love and earth and grant me the position I desire.*

Move quietly back to your workspace and kneel in front of your table. Light your white altar candle and meditate quietly on the Goddess Oshion. Take your coloured spell candle and the small pointed knife and inscribe the number five and the rune symbol Tir at the top of the candle.

Place the candle back in the holder and taking the bottle of empowered oil place some in the palm of your hands. Rub your hands together and visualise that you are charging the energy in the oil and in your hands. Your hands will begin to feel very warm. Take the spell candle and spread the oil from middle to top and middle to bottom of the candle until the candle is completely covered in oil. Visualise that you are empowering the candle with career opportunities. Rub your hands vigorously together with the candle still held between the palms of your hands.

After a few minutes, place your candle back in its holder and light the flame and say these words:

> Work success will come to me –
> Successful now, fulfilled and free.
> I am happy and content
> With this position heaven sent.
> And it harm none so mote it be.

Allow your candle to burn for as long as possible but, if you must put it out, use a candle snuff or pinch the flame between your thumb and finger. You may light your candle again but each time you do so visualise your wish as though it has already begun to happen. When you are finished working clean your hands on the cloth and move quietly to the left of your room.

Extinguish the east candle and say:
> I thank the element of air for blessing me with a new career.

Extinguish the south candle and say:
> I thank the element of fire for blessing me with a new career.

Extinguish the west candle and say:
> I thank the element of water for blessing me with a new career.

Extinguish the north candle and say:
> I thank the element of earth for blessing me with a new career.

Close your circle by saying:
> May the four powers give back to the universe any powers and energies that have not been used.
> The work is now done and the circle is closed.
> So mote it be.

12 Interviews

Day of the week: The best day of the week is Wednesday
Time of day: The best time of day is 5am. Also noon, 7pm or at any time in the evening when the moon is waxing or full but not when it is waning
Goddess: Kali
Guardian Angel: Raphael
Planet: Mercury
Star sign: Gemini or Virgo
Metal: Quicksilver
Colour: Silver or indigo
Rune: Wynn (also known as Wunjo)
Symbol: Papers certificates or official documents
Number: Four, five or seven
Crystal: Amethyst tiger's eye
Flower: Almond blossom
Herb: Dill
Essential Oil: Lemongrass
Tree: Hazel

Mercury

Virgo   Gemini

Wynn

Interviews spell 1

Prepare yourself and decorate your work surface or altar space with all your chosen ingredients such as:

A silver-coloured cloth
A vase of almond blossom
Leaves that have a silver sheen
Your CV
Job adverts or applications
One silver or white taper candle
A piece of amethyst or tiger's eye
One white and one silver taper candle and holders

When you are ready and everything is in place, stand at the edge of your circle. Close your eyes and breathe in, visualising light energy filling your body. Breathe out and breathe away all negative energy. When you are completely relaxed stand up and move quietly to the east quarter of your circle or room.

Light the east candle and say:
  May the element of air bless this space with light, love and air, knowledge and wisdom, so that I may have a successful interview.

Light the south candle and say:
  May the element of fire bless this space with light, love and fire, knowledge and wisdom, so that I may have a successful interview.

Light the west candle and say:
  May the element of water bless this space with light, love and water, knowledge and wisdom, so that I may have a successful interview.

Light the north candle and say:
  May the element of earth bless this space with light, love and earth, knowledge and wisdom, so that I may have a successful interview.

Move quietly back to your workspace and kneel in front of your table. Light your white altar candle and meditate quietly on the Goddess Kali. In your mind see yourself being offered a new position.

Say a prayer in your own words to the Guardian Angel Raphael and stand in front of your altar. Raise your hands high above your head and say these words:

> *Letters dropping on the floor,*
> *Many offers are in store.*
> *The perfect job's within my sight,*
> *My talents, strengths and skills unite.*
> *And it harm none so be it.*

Spend some quiet time in your circle and allow your altar candle to burn through to the end or put it out with a candle snuff. When you are finished working move quietly to the left of your circle.

Extinguish the east candle and say:
> *I thank the element of air for blessing me so that I may have a successful interview.*

Extinguish the south candle and say:
> *I thank the element of fire for blessing me so that I may have a successful interview.*

Extinguish the west candle and say:
> *I thank the element of water for blessing me so that I may have a successful interview.*

Extinguish the north candle and say:
> *I thank the element of earth for blessing me so that I may have a successful interview.*

Close your circle by saying:
> *May the four powers give back to the universe any powers and energies that have not been used.*
> *The work is now done and the circle is closed.*
> *So mote it be.*

Interviews spell 2

10 mls almond oil
Lemongrass pure essential oil
A bottle for your oil mixture
An indigo tablecloth
A small face cloth or some tissues and a small fireproof dish for

matches or burning herbs or paper
Some amethyst crystals
Certificates or qualifications that you have achieved
One white and one silver taper candle and holders
One small pointed knife

Prepare a blend of oils using 10 mls of almond oil and add three drops of lemongrass pure essential oil. Hold the bottle of oil in your hands in the prayer position and rub the bottle vigorously between the palms of your hands and as you do so visualise the oil being empowered with gratitude. When you feel as though the oil has been charged place it on your altar or work surface ready for use along with the other items.

Place four small candles at the east, south, west and north in that order. Sit or kneel comfortably in front of your table. Close your eyes and as you breathe in, picture positive, white light energy filling your body. When you are completely relaxed stand up and move quietly to the east quarter of your room.

Light the east candle and say:
    May the element of air bless this space with light, love and
    air, knowledge and wisdom, so that I may have a successful
    interview

Light the south candle and say:
    May the element of fire bless this space with light, love and
    fire, knowledge and wisdom, so that I may have a success-
    ful interview.

Light the west candle and say:
    May the element of water bless this space with light love
    water, knowledge and wisdom, so that I may have a suc-
    cessful interview.

Light the north candle and say:
    May the element of earth bless this space with light, love
    and earth, knowledge and wisdom, so that I may have a
    successful interview.

Move quietly back to your workspace and kneel in front of your table. Light your white altar candle and meditate quietly on the Goddess Kali. Take your silver spell candle and the small pointed knife and inscribe the number three and the rune symbol Wynn at the top of the candle. Place the candle back in the holder and taking the bottle of empowered oil place some in the palm of your hands. Rub your hands together and visualise that you are charging the energy in the oil and in your hands. Your hands will begin to feel very warm. Take the spell candle and spread the oil from middle to top and middle to bottom of the candle until the candle is completely covered in oil. Visualise that you are empowering the candle with your desire. Rub your hands vigorously together with the candle still held between the palms of your hands. After a few minutes, place your candle back in its holder and light the flame and say these words:

> Candle bring to me the news
> Of successful interviews.
> Happy am I to receive
> Blessings given on this eve.
> And it harm none so mote it be.

Allow your altar candle to burn through to the end or put it out with a candle snuff. You may light your candle again but each time you do so visualise your wish as though it has already begun to happen. When you are finished working, clean your hands on the cloth and move quietly to the left of your room.

Extinguish the east candle and say:
> I thank the element of air for blessing me so that I may have a successful interview.

Extinguish the south candle and say:
> I thank the element of fire for blessing me so that I may have a successful interview.

Extinguish the west candle and say:
> I thank the element of water for blessing me so that I may have a successful interview.

Extinguish the north candle and say:
> I thank the element of earth for blessing me so that I may have a successful interview.

Close your circle by saying:
> May the four powers give back to the universe any powers and energies that have not been used.
> The work is now done and the circle is closed.
> So mote it be.

13 Protection

Day of the week: The best day of the week is Thursday
Time of day: The best time of day 5am. Also noon, 7pm or at any time in the evening when the moon is waxing or full but not when it is waning
Goddess: Callisto
Planet: Jupiter
Guardian angel: Zadkiel
Star sign: Sagittarius
Metal: Tin
Colour: Blue
Rune: Eohl
Symbol: Ankh
Number: Eight
Crystal: Turquoise
Flower: Lilac and apple blossom
Essential oil: Frankincense
Herb: Garlic, mint or feverfew
Tree: Rowan

Jupiter

Sagittarius

An Egyptian ankh

Eohl

Protection spell 1

Prepare yourself and decorate your work surface or altar space with all your chosen ingredients such as:

An ankh, or a crucifix
One white and one blue taper candle and holders
A clove of garlic
A vase of lilac flowers
A dish of salt and a small bowl of water
A dish containing some dried or fresh mint
A sprig of rowan
A piece of turquoise

When you are ready and everything is in place, stand at the edge of your circle. Close your eyes and breathe in, visualising light energy filling your body. Breathe out and breathe away all negative energy. When you are completely relaxed stand up and move quietly to the east quarter of your circle or room.

Light the east candle and say:
> May the element of air bless this space with light, love and air and grant me protection in everything I do and anywhere I go.

Light the south candle and say:
> May the element of fire bless this space with light, love and fire and grant me protection in everything I do and anywhere I go.

Light the west candle and say:
> May the element of water bless this space with light, love and water and grant me protection in everything I do and anywhere I go.

Light the north candle and say:
> May the element of earth bless this space with light, love and earth and grant me protection in everything I do and anywhere I go.

Move quietly back to your workspace, kneel in front of your table and light your white altar candle.
    Place the dish of water in front of you and take three pinches of salt

and add this to the water dish. Raise your dominant hand high above your head pointing your index finger to the sky above you. Visualise white light connecting with your index finger and flowing through your body.

Now place your index finger into the dish of salted water and saw these words:

> Water be healing and salt be pure
> Keep me safe and protected sure.
> Guard me and mine from any harm,
> Whilst I keep this sacred charm.
> Bad energy please turn from me
> Send it back so none need flee.
> And it harm none so mote it be.

Dip the ankh or crucifix once in the salted water.

Spend some time meditating quietly on the Goddess Callisto and allow your altar candle to burn through to the end, or put it out with a candle snuff or pinch the wick between dampened fingertips.

When you are finished working move quietly to the left of your circle.

Extinguish the east candle and say:
> I thank the element of air for blessing me with protection, making me and mine safe in everything that we do or anywhere that we go.

Extinguish the south candle and say:
> I thank the element of fire for blessing me with protection, making me and mine safe in everything that we do or anywhere that we go.

Extinguish the west candle and say:
> I thank the element of water for blessing me with protection, making me and mine safe in everything that we do or anywhere that we go.

Extinguish the north candle and say:
> I thank the element of earth for blessing me with protection, making me and mine safe in everything that we do or anywhere that we go.

Close your circle by saying:
> May the four powers give back to the universe any powers

and energies that have not been used.
The work is now done and the circle is closed.
So mote it be.

Wear the ankh or crucifix round your neck or keep it safe on your person. Take your dish of water and salt and go to your front door. Holding the dish in your non-dominant hand place the fingers of your dominant hand in the dish and flick the salted water around your door. Do this round the walls and the windows and, if you have a garden, sprinkle the water round the perimeter of your garden. This can also be done on your car. Do not forget to sprinkle some on your letterbox and your telephone. As you sprinkle be sure to repeat the words:

> Water be healing and salt be pure
> Keep me safe and protected sure.
> Guard me and mine from any harm
> Whilst I keep this sacred charm.
> Bad energy please turn from me
> Send it back so none need flee.
> And it harm none so mote it be.

If you run out of water and salt make some more. You do not have to cast a circle to do this but you should visualise the connection to the pure energy from infinity above you before you begin.

Protection spell 2

10 mls almond oil
Frankincense pure essential oil
A bottle for your oil mixture
A small face cloth or some tissues
A small fireproof dish for matches or burning herbs or paper
An ankh or crucifix
A vase of apple blossom
A piece of turquoise
One tall blue and one tall white taper candle and holders
One small pointed knife

Prepare a blend of oils using 10 mls of almond oil and add three drops of frankincense pure essential oil. Hold the bottle of oil in your hands in the prayer position and rub the bottle vigorously between the palms of your hands and as you do so visualise the oil being empowered with the power of protection. When you feel as though the oil has been charged, place it on your altar or work surface, ready for use along with the other items.

Place four small candles at the east, south, west, and north in that order.

Sit or kneel comfortably in front of your table. Close your eyes and as you breathe in, picture positive, white light energy filling your body. When you are completely relaxed, stand up and move quietly to the east quarter of your room.

Light the east candle and say:

>*May the element of air bless this space with light, love and air and grant me protection in everything I do and anywhere I go.*

Light the south candle and say:

>*May the element of fire bless this space with light, love and fire and grant me protection in everything I do and anywhere I go.*

Light the west candle and say:

>*May the element of water bless this space with light, love and water and grant me protection in everything I do and anywhere I go.*

Light the north candle and say:

>*May the element of earth bless this space with light, love and earth and grant me protection in everything I do and anywhere I go.*

Move quietly back to your workspace and kneel in front of your table. Light your white altar candle and meditate quietly on the Goddess Callisto. Take your blue spell candle and the small pointed knife and inscribe the number eight and the rune symbol Eohl at the top of the candle. Place the candle back in the holder and, taking the bottle of empowered oil, place some in the palm of your hands.

Rub your hands together and visualise that you are charging the energy in the oil and in your hands. Your hands will begin to feel very warm. Take the spell candle and spread the oil from middle to top and middle to bottom of the candle until the candle is completely covered in oil.

Visualise that you are empowering the candle with the power of protection. Rub your hands vigorously together with the candle still held between the palms of your hands. After a few minutes, place your candle back in its holder and light the flame and say these words:

> Flame that burns and brings me light
> Keep me safe both day and night.
> Even when the flame is done
> Let no harm come from any one.
> And it harm none so mote it be.

Allow your candle to burn for as long as possible or use a candle snuff to put it out. You may light your candle again but each time you do so visualise your wish as though it has already begun to happen. When you are finished working, clean your hands on the cloth and move quietly to the left of your room.

Extinguish the east candle and say:
> I thank the element of air for blessing me with protection, making me and mine safe in everything that we do or anywhere that we go.

Extinguish the south candle and say:
> I thank the element of fire for blessing me with protection, making me and mine safe in everything that we do or anywhere that we go.

Extinguish the west candle and say:
> I thank the element of water for blessing me with protection, making me and mine safe in everything that we do or anywhere that we go.

Extinguish the north candle and say:
> I thank the element of earth for blessing me with protection, making me and mine safe in everything that we do or anywhere that we go.

Close your circle by saying:
> May the four powers give back to the universe any powers and energies that have not been used.
> The work is now done and the circle is closed.
> So mote it be.

For as long as you feel threatened light a candle each day or night and as you light the flame say the words:

Flame that burns and brings me light
Keep me safe both day and night.
Even when the flame is done
Let no harm come from anyone.
And it harm none so mote it be.

14 Opportunities

Day of the week: The best day of the week is Sunday
Time of day: The best time of day 5am. Also noon, 7pm or at any time in the evening when the moon is waxing or full but not when it is waning
Goddess: Carna
Planet: Sun
Star sign: Leo
Metal: Gold
Colour: Yellow
Rune: Ken (also known as Kano), Daeg (also known as Dagaz)
Symbol: Keys and doors
Number: Seven
Crystal: Diamond, ruby, sun stone or citrine
Flower: Jasmine
Essential oil: Neroli
Tree: Cherry

Sun

Leo

Ken   Dagaz

Opportunity spell 1

Prepare yourself and decorate your work surface or altar space with all your chosen ingredients such as:

Yellow and gold coloured cloths
A letter addressed to yourself or for whomever you are preparing the spell. [In the letter write the words. 'We would like to offer you (insert your own words here)']
Diamond or ruby jewellery, citrine or sunstone crystals
Circular shaped discs covered with gold foil to represent the sun
One gold and one white taper candle and holders
An ashtray or a small fireproof dish
Some matches or a lighter
A vase of jasmine blossoms

When you are ready and everything is in place, stand at the edge of your circle. Close your eyes and breathe in, visualising light energy filling your body. Breathe out and breathe away all negative energy. When you are completely relaxed stand up and move quietly to the east quarter of your circle or room.

Light the east candle and say:
    May the element of air bless this space with light, love and air and grant me the opportunity to change my life for the better.

Light the south candle and say:
    May the element of fire bless this space with light, love and fire and grant me the opportunity to change my life for the better.

Light the west candle and say:
    May the element of water bless this space with light, love and water and grant me the opportunity to change my life for the better.

Light the north candle and say:
    May the element of earth bless this space with light, love and earth and grant me the opportunity to change my life for the better.

Move quietly back to your workspace and kneel in front of your table.

Light your white altar candle and meditate quietly on the Goddess Carna. In your mind give thanks for the gifts that you have been given.

Open your letter and read aloud the words that you have written and in your mind visualise this coming true. Light your gold candle and light the letter from the gold candle and allow it to burn through in the fireproof dish.

Stand in front of your altar, raise your hands high above your head and say these words:

> Carna hear me when I say
> I give thanks to you today
> Chances offered I will take
> And my future I shall make
> And it harm none so be it.

Spend some quiet time in your circle and allow your altar candle to burn through to the end or put it out with a candle snuff. When you are finished working, move quietly to the left of your circle.

Extinguish the east candle and say:
   I thank the element of air for blessing me with the opportunity to change my life.

Extinguish the south candle and say:
   I thank the element of fire for blessing me with the opportunity to change my life.

Extinguish the west candle and say:
   I thank the element of water for blessing me with the opportunity to change my life.

Extinguish the north candle and say:
   I thank the element of earth for blessing me with the opportunity to change my life.

Close your circle by saying:
   May the four powers give back to the universe any powers and energies that have not been used.
   The work is now done and the circle is closed.
   So mote it be.

Opportunity spell 2

10 mls almond oil
Neroli pure essential oil
A bottle for your oil mixture
A small face cloth or some tissues
A small fireproof dish for matches or burning herbs or paper
An incense burner to which you have added yellow or gold col-
    oured potpourri and a few drops of your favourite oil
A piece of sun stone
One tall white and one tall yellow or gold taper candle and
    holders
One small pointed knife

Prepare a blend of oils using 10 mls of almond oil and add three drops
of neroli pure essential oil. Hold the bottle of oil in your hands in the
prayer position and rub the bottle vigorously between the palms of
your hands and as you do so visualise the oil being empowered with
gratitude. When you feel as though the oil has been charged place it
on your altar or work surface ready for use along with the other items.

Place four small candles at the east, south, west and north in that
order. Sit or kneel comfortably in front of your table. Close your eyes
and, as you breathe in, picture positive white light energy filling your
body. When you are completely relaxed stand up and move quietly to
the east quarter of your room.

Light the east candle and say:
    *May the element of air bless this space with light, love and
    air and grant me the opportunity to change my life for the
    better.*

Light the south candle and say:
    *May the element of fire bless this space with light, love and
    fire and grant me the opportunity to change my life for the
    better.*

Light the west candle and say:
    *May the element of water bless this space with light, love
    and water and grant me the opportunity to change my life
    for the better.*

Light the north candle and say:
> May the element of earth bless this space with light, love
> and earth and grant me the opportunity to change my life
> for the better.

Move quietly back to your workspace and kneel in front of your table. Light your white altar candle and meditate quietly on the opportunities that you would like to see come your way. Take your yellow or gold spell candle and the small pointed knife and inscribe the number seven and the rune symbol Daeg at the top of the candle. Place the candle back in the holder and, taking the bottle of empowered oil, place some in the palm of your hands. Rub your hands together and visualise that you are charging the energy in the oil and in your hands. Your hands will begin to feel very warm. Take the spell candle and spread the oil from middle to top and middle to bottom of the candle until the candle is completely covered in oil. Visualise that you are empowering the candle with exciting new opportunities. Rub your hands vigorously together with the candle still held between the palms of your hands.

After a few minutes, place your spell candle back in its holder and light the flame and say these words:

> Chances now have come my way,
> Blessed be this special day.
> My life is changed, improving ever,
> Chances now do come together.
> And it harm none so mote it be.

Allow your altar candle to burn through to the end or put it out with a candle snuff. You may light your candle again but each time you do so visualise your wish as though it has already begun to happen. When you are finished working clean your hands on the cloth and move quietly to the left of your room.

Extinguish the east candle and say:
> I thank the element of air for blessing me with the opportu-
> nity to change my life.

Extinguish the south candle and say:
> I thank the element of fire for blessing me with the oppor-
> tunity to change my life.

Extinguish the west candle and say:
>   I thank the element of water for blessing me with the opportunity to change my life.

Extinguish the north candle and say:
>   I thank the element of earth for blessing me with the opportunity to change my life.

Close your circle by saying:
>   May the four powers give back to the universe any powers and energies that have not been used.
>   The work is now done and the circle is closed.
>   So mote it be.

15 Marriage

Day of the week: The best day of the week is Friday

Time of day: The best time of day is 5am. Also noon, 7pm or at any time in the evening when the moon is waxing or full but not when it is waning

Goddess: Freya

Planet: Venus

Guardian Angel: Adonai

Star sign: Taurus and Libra

Metal: Rose, gold and copper

Colour: Red, pink or green

Rune: Geofu (also known as Gefu), Ing (also known as Ingux, Ingwaz), Mann (also known as Manaz)

Symbol: Rings

Number: Two, four and six

Crystal: Rose quartz

Flower: Rose

Essential Oil: Rose otto

Tree: Apple

Herb: Ylang ylang

Venus

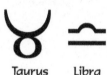

Taurus   Libra

Geofu   Ing

Mann

Marriage spell 1

Prepare yourself and decorate your work surface or altar space with all your chosen ingredients such as:

Cloths, which are coloured red, pink and green
Place on your table pieces of paper on which you have written
  the numbers two, four and six
Several pieces of rose quartz
A dish in which you have placed some rings
One white and one pink taper candle and holders
A small posy of pink roses

When you are ready and everything is in place, stand at the edge of your circle. Close your eyes and breathe in, visualising light energy filling your body. Breathe out and breathe away all negative energy.

When you are completely relaxed, stand up and move quietly to the east quarter of your circle or room.

Light the east candle and say:
  May the element of air bless this space with light, love and
  air and bless our sacred union so that we may live long and
  happy together.

Light the south candle and say:
  May the element of fire bless this space with light, love and
  fire and bless our sacred union so that we may live long and
  happy together.

Light the west candle and say:
  May the element of water bless this space with light, love
  and water and bless our sacred union so that we may live
  long and happy together.

Light the north candle and say:
  May the element of earth bless this space with light, love
  and earth and bless our sacred union so that we may live
  long and happy together.

Move quietly back to your workspace and kneel in front of your table. Light your white altar candle and meditate quietly on the Goddess Venus. Say a prayer in your own words to the Guardian Angel Adonai.

Light your pink candle and stand in front of your altar, raise your hands high above your head and say these words:

> Marriage is a sacred way.
> None shall come between us
> Blessed with love every day
> This our gift from Venus.
> And it harm none so be it.

Spend some quiet time in your circle and allow your altar candle to burn through to the end or put it out with a candle snuff. When you are finished working move quietly to the left of your circle.

Extinguish the east candle and say:
> I thank the element of air for blessing our union so that we may live long and happy together.

Extinguish the south candle and say:
> I thank the element of fire for blessing our union so that we may live long and happy together.

Extinguish the west candle and say:
> I thank the element of water for blessing our union so that we may live long and happy together.

Extinguish the north candle and say:
> I thank the element of earth for blessing our union so that we may live long and happy together.

Close your circle by saying
> May the four powers give back to the universe any powers and energies that have not been used.
> The work is now done and the circle is closed.
> So mote it be.

Marriage spell 2

10 mls almond oil
Rose otto pure essential oil
A bottle for your oil mixture
A small face cloth or some tissues
A small fireproof dish for matches or burning herbs or paper
Write on a piece of paper the words: 'May (name) and I live long

and happy lives together blessed with perfect love, perfect
truth and perfect happiness'
Photographs of happily married couples (You could use pho-
tographs that are personal to you such as parents or
grandparents)
Some rose quartz
One white and one pink candle and holders
One small pointed knife

Prepare a blend of oils using 10 mls of almond oil and add three drops
of rose otto pure essential oil. Hold the bottle of oil in your hands in
the prayer position and rub the bottle vigorously between the palms
of your hands and as you do so visualise the oil being empowered with
gratitude. When you feel as though the oil has been charged, place it
on your altar or work surface ready for use along with the other items.

Place four small candles at the east, south, west and north in that
order.

Sit or kneel comfortably in front of your table. Close your eyes and
as you breathe in, picture positive, white light energy filling your body.
When you are completely relaxed stand up and move quietly to the
east quarter of your room.

Light the east candle and say:

*May the element of air bless this space with light, love and
air and bless our sacred union so that we may live long and
happy together.*

Light the south candle and say:

*May the element of fire bless this space with light, love and
fire and bless our sacred union so that we may live long and
happy together.*

Light the west candle and say:

*May the element of water bless this space with light, love
and water and bless our sacred union so that we may live
long and happy together.*

Light the north candle and say:

*May the element of earth bless this space with light, love
and earth and bless our sacred union so that we may live
long and happy together.*

Move quietly back to your workspace and kneel in front of your table. Light your white altar candle and meditate quietly on you and your partner and the life that you see ahead of you. Take your pink spell candle and the small pointed knife and inscribe the numbers two, four and six and the rune symbol Geofu and Ing at the top of the candle. Place the candle back in the holder and, taking the bottle of empowered oil, place some in the palms of your hands. Rub your hands together and visualise that you are charging the energy in the oil and in your hands. Your hands will begin to feel very warm. Take the spell candle and spread the oil from middle to top and middle to bottom of the candle until the candle is completely covered in oil. Visualise that you are empowering the candle with stability and security in your marriage. Rub your hands vigorously together with the candle still held between the palms of your hands. After a few minutes, place your candle back in its holder and light the flame and say these words:

> I give myself to you in love,
> Promises we make forever.
> Blessed by all the stars above,
> Remembered always – forgotten never.
> And it harm none so mote it be.

Take the paper that you have written on and light it with the pink candle. Let it burn through in the fireproof dish. Allow your altar candles to burn through to the end or put them out with a candle snuff. You may light your candles again but each time you do so visualise your wish as though it has already begun to happen. When you are finished working, clean your hands on the cloth and move quietly to the left of your room.

Extinguish the east candle and say:
> I thank the element of air for blessing our union so that we may live long and happily together.

Extinguish the south candle and say:
> I thank the element of fire for blessing our union so that we may live long and happily together.

Extinguish the west candle and say:
> I thank the element of water for blessing our union so that we may live long and happily together.

Extinguish the north candle and say:
    I thank the element of earth for blessing our union so that
    we may live long and happily together.

Close your circle by saying;
    May the four powers give back to the universe any powers
    and energies that have not been used.
    The work is now done and the circle is closed.
    So mote it be.

16 Harvest

Day of the week: The best day of the week is Saturday
Time of day: The best time of day is 5am. Also noon, 7pm or at any time in the evening when the moon is waxing or full but not when it is waning
Goddess: Ceres
Planet: Saturn
Star sign: Capricorn
Metal: Lead
Colour: Deep blue
Rune: Jara (also known as Jera)
Symbol: Autumn leaves, wheat sheaves, grains or bread
Number: Nine
Crystal: Lapis or amber
Flower: Violet
Essential oil: Sage
Tree: Bamboo

Saturn

Capricorn

Jara

Harvest spell 1

Prepare yourself and decorate your work surface or altar space with all your chosen ingredients such as:

A deep blue cloth
Some autumn coloured leaves and a small bamboo plant (available from most garden stores)
A piece of amber or lapis
One gold and one white taper candle and holders
Some crusty bread
A dish of grains or cereals

When you are ready and everything is in place, stand at the edge of your circle. Close your eyes and breathe in, visualising light energy filling your body. Breathe out and breathe away all negative energy. When you are completely relaxed stand up and move quietly to the east quarter of your circle or room.

Light the east candle and say:
    May the element of air bless this space with light, love and air and bless the work that I have done so that I may reap the rewards for my efforts.

Light the south candle and say:
    May the element of fire bless this space with light, love and fire and bless the work that I have done so that I may reap the rewards for my efforts.

Light the west candle and say:
    May the element of water bless this space with light, love and water and bless the work that I have done so that I may reap the rewards for my efforts.

Light the north candle and say:
    May the element of earth bless this space with light, love and earth and bless the work that I have done so that I may reap the rewards for my efforts.

Move quietly back to your workspace and kneel in front of your table. Light your white altar candle and meditate quietly on the Goddess Ceres. In your mind give thanks for the ability to work and see your rewards grow before you. Break a piece from the crusty bread and eat it, enjoying the taste and savouring every mouthful. Think about how this piece of bread came to be, starting with the planting of the seed. See the seed growing and dancing in a gentle breeze. Say a prayer in your own words to your Guardian Angel. Stand in front of your altar, raise your hands high above your head and say these words:

> *Seeds where planted now they grow,*
> *Rewards to me begin to flow,*
> *Harvest time comes round again*
> *Blessed by sun and wind and rain.*
> *And it harm none so be it.*

Spend some quiet time in your circle and allow your altar candle to burn through to the end or put it out with a candle snuff. When you are finished working, move quietly to the left of your circle.

Extinguish the east candle and say:
> *I thank the element of air for blessing the work that I have done so that I may reap the rewards for my efforts.*

Extinguish the south candle and say:
> *I thank the element of fire for blessing the work that I have done so that I may reap the rewards for my efforts.*

Extinguish the west candle and say:
> *I thank the element of water for blessing the work that I have done so that I may reap the rewards for my efforts.*

Extinguish the north candle and say:
> *I thank the element of earth for blessing the work that I have done so that I may reap the rewards for my efforts.*

Close your circle by saying:
> *May the four powers give back to the universe any powers and energies that have not been used.*
> *The work is now done and the circle is closed.*
> *So mote it be.*

Harvest spell 2

10 mls almond oil
Sage pure essential oil
A bottle for your oil mixture
A small face cloth or some tissues and a small fireproof dish for
    matches or burning herbs or paper.
A golden cloth
A vase of violets
A piece of lead
One white and one deep blue candle and holders

Prepare a blend of oils using 10 mls of almond oil and add three drops
of sage pure essential oil. Hold the bottle of oil in your hands in the
prayer position and rub the bottle vigorously between the palms of
your hands and as you do so visualise the oil being empowered with
gratitude. When you feel as though the oil has been charged place it
on your altar or work surface ready for use along with the other items.

Place four small candles at the east, south, west and north in that
order. Sit or kneel comfortably in front of your table. Close your eyes
and, as you breathe in, picture positive white light energy filling your
body. When you are completely relaxed, stand up and move quietly
to the east quarter of your room.

Light the east candle and say:
  *May the element of air bless this space with light, love and
  air and bless the work that I have done so that I may reap
  the rewards for my efforts.*

Light the south candle and say:
  *May the element of fire bless this space with light, love and
  fire and bless the work that I have done so that I may reap
  the rewards for my efforts.*

Light the west candle and say:
  *May the element of water bless this space with light, love
  and water and bless the work that I have done so that I may
  reap the rewards for my efforts.*

Light the north candle and say:
  *May the element of earth bless this space with light, love
  and earth and bless the work that I have done so that I may
  reap the rewards for my efforts.*

Move quietly back to your workspace and kneel in front of your table. Light your white altar candle and meditate quietly on the work that you have done and the rewards that you are hoping to achieve. Take your blue spell candle and the small pointed knife and inscribe the number nine and the rune symbol Jara at the top of the candle. Place the candle back in the holder and taking the bottle of empowered oil place some in the palm of your hands. Rub your hands together and visualise that you are charging the energy in the oil and in your hands. Your hands will begin to feel very warm. Take the spell candle and spread the oil from middle to top and middle to bottom of the candle until the candle is completely covered in oil. Visualise that you are empowering the candle with a bountiful harvest. Rub your hands vigorously together with the candle still held between the palms of your hands. After a few minutes, place your candle back in its holder and light the flame and say these words.

> Candle burning clear and bright,
> I have worked from day till night,
> The fruits of work begin to show,
> Make them golden, let them grow.
> And it harm none so mote it be.

Allow your altar candles to burn through to the end or put them out with a candle snuff. You may light your candles again but each time you do so visualise your wish as though it has already begun to happen. When you are finished working, clean your hands on the cloth and move quietly to the left of your room.

Extinguish the east candle and say:
> I thank the element of air for blessing the work that I have done so that I may reap the rewards for my efforts.

Extinguish the south candle and say:
> I thank the element of fire for blessing the work that I have done so that I may reap the rewards for my efforts.

Extinguish the west candle and say:
> I thank the element of water for blessing the work that I have done so that I may reap the rewards for my efforts.

Extinguish the north candle and say:
> I thank the element of earth for blessing the work that I have done so that I may reap the rewards for my efforts.

Close your circle by saying:
    May the four powers give back to the universe any powers
    and energies that have not been used.
    The work is now done and the circle is closed.
    So mote it be.

17 Secrets

Day of the week: The best day of the week is Tuesday
Time of day: The best time of day is 5am. Also noon, 7pm or at any time in the evening when the moon is waxing or full but not when it is waning
Goddess: Meretsegar
Guardian Angel: Masleh
Planet: Pluto
Star sign: Scorpio
Metal: Tungsten or tutonium
Colour: Black
Rune: Peorth
Symbol: Diaries, puzzles or boxes
Number: Two
Crystal: Beryl or sardonyx
Flower: Begonia
Essential oil: Geranium
Herb: Coriander
Tree: Cedar

Pluto

Scorpio

Peorth

Secrets spell 1

Prepare yourself and decorate your work surface or altar space with all your chosen ingredients such as:

A black silk or velvet cloth
On your table place an incense burner to which you have added some water and a pinch of dried coriander and some geranium or cedar essential oil
A piece of beryl, sardonyx, jet or obsidian
Your diary and some puzzles
One white and one black tall taper candle and holders

When you are ready and everything is in place, stand at the edge of your circle. Close your eyes and breathe in, visualising light energy filling your body. Breathe out and breathe away all negative energy. When you are completely relaxed stand up and move quietly to the east quarter of your circle or room.

Light the east candle and say:
    May the element of air bless this space with light, love and
    air and keep my secret so that none may share.

Light the south candle and say:
    May the element of fire bless this space with light, love and
    fire and keep my secret so that none may share.

Light the west candle and say:
    May the element of water bless this space with light, love and
    water and keep my secret so that none may share.

Light the north candle and say:
    May the element of earth bless this space with light, love and
    earth and keep my secret so that none may share.

Move quietly back to your workspace and kneel in front of your table. Light your white altar candle and meditate quietly on the Goddess Meretsegar. In your mind, visualise your secret being locked into a small black box. Say a prayer in your own words to the Guardian Angel Masleh and stand in front of your altar. Raise your hands high above your head and say these words:

In my heart I hold the key
To the secret none should see.
Never will it be revealed
Blessed be the powers that be.
And it harm none so be it.

Light your black candle and meditate as the candle burns. See in your mind the secret being consumed by the flame. Spend some quiet time in your circle and allow your altar candles to burn through to the end or put them out with a candle snuff. When you are finished working, move quietly to the left of your circle.

Extinguish the east candle and say:
    I thank the element of air for blessing and keeping my secret so that none may share.

Extinguish the south candle and say:
    I thank the element of fire for blessing and keeping my secret so that none may share.

Extinguish the west candle and say:
    I thank the element of water for blessing and keeping my secret so that none may share.

Extinguish the north candle and say:
    I thank the element of earth for blessing and keeping my secret so that none may share.

Close your circle by saying:
    May the four powers give back to the universe any powers and energies that have not been used.
    The work is now done and the circle is closed.
    So mote it be.

Secrets spell 2

10 mls almond oil
Geranium pure essential oil
A bottle for your oil mixture
A small face cloth or some tissues
A small fireproof dish for matches or burning herbs or paper
A black silk or velvet cloth to cover your table with
A single begonia in a black vase

Some black coloured crystals
One white and one black taper candle and holders
A small sharp knife

Prepare a blend of oils using 10 mls of almond oil and add three drops
of geranium pure essential oil. Hold the bottle of oil in your hands in
the prayer position and rub the bottle vigorously between the palms
of your hands and as you do so visualise the oil being empowered with
gratitude. When you feel as though the oil has been charged place it
on your altar or work surface ready for use along with the other items.

Place four small candles at the east, south, west and north in that
order. Sit or kneel comfortably in front of your table. Close your eyes
and as you breathe in, picture positive white light energy filling your
body. When you are completely relaxed stand up and move quietly to
the east quarter of your room.

Light the east candle and say:
    *May the element of air bless this space with light, love and
    air and keep my secret so that none may share.*

Light the south candle and say:
    *May the element of fire bless this space with light, love and
    fire and keep my secret so that none may share.*

Light the west candle and say:
    *May the element of water bless this space with light, love and
    water and keep my secret so that none may share.*

Light the north candle and say:
    *May the element of earth bless this space with light, love and
    earth and keep my secret so that none may share.*

Move quietly back to your workspace and kneel in front of your table.
Light your white altar candle and meditate quietly on your secret. Take
your black spell candle and the small pointed knife and inscribe the
number two and the rune symbol Peorth at the top of the candle. Place
the candle back in the holder and taking the bottle of empowered oil
place some in the palm of your hands. Rub your hands together and
visualise that you are charging the energy in the oil and in your hands.
Your hands will begin to feel very warm.

Take the spell candle and spread the oil from middle to top and
middle to bottom of the candle until the candle is completely covered
in oil. Visualise that you are empowering the candle with hidden

information. Rub your hands vigorously together with the candle still held between the palms of your hands.

After a few minutes, place your candle back in its holder and light the flame and say these words:

> To the candle burning bright
> I give my secret here tonight.
> None shall listen, none shall see,
> Just the candle, flame and me.
> And it harm none so mote it be.

Allow your altar candle to burn through to the end or put it out with a candle snuff. You may light your candles again but each time you do so, visualise your wish as though it has already begun to happen. When you are finished working, clean your hands on the cloth and move quietly to the left of your room.

Extinguish the east candle and say:
>   I thank the element of air for blessing and keeping my secret so that none may share.

Extinguish the south candle and say:
>   I thank the element of fire for blessing and keeping my secret so that none may share.

Extinguish the west candle and say:
>   I thank the element of water for blessing and keeping my secret so that none may share.

Extinguish the north candle and say:
>   I thank the element of earth for blessing and keeping my secret so that none may share.

Close your circle by saying:
>   May the four powers give back to the universe any powers and energies that have not been used.
>   The work is now done and the circle is closed.
>   So mote it be.

18 Home

Day of the week: The best day of the week is Monday
Time of day: The best time of day is 5am. Also noon, 7pm or at any time in the evening when the moon is waxing or full but not when it is waning
Goddess: Heket
Planet: Moon
Guardian Angel: Haniel
Star sign: Cancer or Taurus
Metal: Silver or gold
Colour: Green or gold or silver
Rune: Othel
Symbol: Hand-knitted or hand-sewn items, cakes and breads
Number: Four
Crystal: Rhodochrosite
Flower: Honeysuckle
Essential oil: Jasmine
Tree: Rowan
Herb: Myrrh

Moon

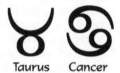

Taurus   Cancer

Othel

Home spell 1

Prepare yourself and decorate your work surface or altar space with all your chosen ingredients such as:

A green cloth and some small frog ornaments
Some small kitchen tools
Hand-sewn or hand-knitted items
A piece of rhodochrosite
One green and one white taper candle and holders
A vase of honeysuckle
A bowl of fruit
A sprig of rowan
A piece of rhodochrosite crystal

When you are ready and everything is in place, stand at the edge of your circle. Close your eyes and breathe in, visualising light energy filling your body. Breathe out and breathe away all negative energy. When you are completely relaxed stand up and move quietly to the east quarter of your circle or room.

Light the east candle and say:
  May the element of air bless this space with light, love and air and keep my home safe and happy.

Light the south candle and say:
  May the element of fire bless this space with light, love and fire and keep my home safe and happy.

Light the west candle and say:
  May the element of water bless this space with light, love and water and keep my home safe and happy.

Light the north candle and say:
  May the element of earth bless this space with light, love and earth and keep my home safe and happy.

Move quietly back to your workspace and kneel in front of your table. Light your white altar candle and meditate quietly on the Goddess Heket. In your mind, see your home happy, contended and safe and blessed with abundance. Say a prayer in your own words to the Guardian Angel Haniel. Stand in front of your altar, raise your hands high above your head and say these words:

> Happy is the home I have,
> Contented is the life I live,
> Blessed is the joy I share,
> Blessed by Heket who doth care.
> And it harm none so be it.

Spend some quiet time in your circle and allow your altar candle to burn through to the end but if you must put it out do so with a candle snuff or pinch the wick between dampened fingertips.

When you are finished working move quietly to the left of your circle.

Extinguish the east candle and say:
> I thank the element of air for blessing me so that I may have a happy home.

Extinguish the south candle and say:
> I thank the element of fire for blessing me so that I may have a happy home.

Extinguish the west candle and say:
> I thank the element of water for blessing me so that I may have a happy home.

Extinguish the north candle and say:
> I thank the element of earth for blessing me so that I may have a happy home.

Close your circle by saying:
> May the four powers give back to the universe any powers and energies that have not been used.
> The work is now done and the circle is closed.
> So mote it be.

Home spell 2

10 mls almond oil
Myrrh pure essential oil
A bottle for your oil mixture
A green tablecloth
A small face cloth or some tissues
A small fireproof dish for matches or burning herbs or paper.
One white and one green taper candle and holders
One small pointed knife

Some small, favourite household items
A rhodochrosite crystal
A small dish containing some dried basil

Prepare a blend of oils using 10 mls of almond oil and add three drops of myrrh pure essential oil. Hold the bottle of oil in your hands in the prayer position and rub the bottle vigorously between the palms of your hands and as you do so visualise the oil being empowered with gratitude. When you feel as though the oil has been charged place it on your altar or work surface ready for use along with the other items. Place four small candles at the east, south, west and north in that order.

Sit or kneel comfortably in front of your table. Close your eyes and as you breathe in, picture positive white light energy filling your body.

When you are completely relaxed stand up and move quietly to the east quarter of your room.

Light the east candle and say:
   May the element of air bless this space with light, love and air and keep my home safe and happy.

Light the south candle and say:
   May the element of fire bless this space with light, love and fire and keep my home safe and happy.

Light the west candle and say:
   May the element of water bless this space with light, love and water and keep my home safe and happy.

Light the north candle and say:
   May the element of earth bless this space with light, love and earth and keep my home safe and happy.

Move quietly back to your workspace and kneel in front of your table. Light your white altar candle and meditate quietly on your home. Take your green spell candle and the small pointed knife and inscribe the number four and the rune symbol Othel at the top of the candle. Place the candle back in the holder and taking the bottle of empowered oil place some in the palm of your hands. Rub your hands together and visualise that you are charging the energy in the oil and in your hands. Your hands will begin to feel very warm. Take the spell candle and spread the oil from middle to top and middle to bottom of the candle until the candle is completely covered in oil. Visualise that you are empowering your candle with a happy and contented home.

Rub your hands vigorously together with the candle still held between the palms of your hands. After a few minutes, place your candle back in its holder and light the flame and say these words:

> Enter here within my home,
> Witness here the love that's shown.
> Content and happy, safe and warm,
> Safe from any outside harm.
> And it harm none so mote it be.

Allow your altar candle to burn through to the end or put it out with a candle snuff. You may light your candle again but, each time you do so, visualise your wish as though it has already begun to happen. When you are finished working clean your hands on the cloth and move quietly to the left of your room.

Extinguish the east candle and say:
> I thank the element of air for blessing me so that I may have a happy home.

Extinguish the south candle and say:
> I thank the element of fire for blessing me so that I may have a happy home.

Extinguish the west candle and say:
> I thank the element of water for blessing me so that I may have a happy home.

Extinguish the north candle and say:
> I thank the element of earth for blessing me so that I may have a happy home.

Close your circle by saying:
> May the four powers give back to the universe any powers and energies that have not been used.
> The work is now done and the circle is closed.
> So mote it be.

19 Fertility

Day of the week: The best day of the week is Friday
Time of day: The best time of day is 5am. Also noon, 7pm or at any time in the evening when the moon is waxing or full but not when it is waning
Goddess: Vesta
Planet: Mars or Venus
Guardian Angel: Raziel
Star sign: Scorpio
Metal: Iron
Colour: Red
Rune: Beork, Wynn (also known as Wunjo)
Symbol: Eggs
Number: One and three
Crystal: Moonstone and carnelian
Flower: Hyacinth
Essential oil: Frankincense
Herb: Mint
Tree: Birch

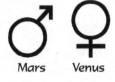

Mars   Venus

Scorpio

Beork   Wynn

Fertility spell

Prepare yourself and decorate your work surface or altar space with all your chosen ingredients such as:

A red coloured cloth
A bowl of wooden or marble eggs
One red and one white taper candle and holders
A vase of hyacinth flowers
A bowl of apples
Some moonstone or carnelian crystals
A piece of iron

When you are ready and everything is in place, stand at the edge of your circle. Close your eyes and breathe in, visualising light energy filling your body. Breathe out and breathe away all negative energy. When you are completely relaxed, stand up and move quietly to the east quarter of your circle or room.

Light the east candle and say:
  May the element of air bless this space with light, love and air and make me fertile

Light the south candle and say:
  May the element of fire bless this space with light, love and fire and make me fertile

Light the west candle and say:
  May the element of water bless this space with light, love and water and make me fertile.

Light the north candle and say:
  May the element of earth bless this space with light, love and earth and make me fertile.

Move quietly back to your workspace and kneel in front of your table. Light your white altar candle and meditate quietly on the Goddess Vesta. In your mind see yourself holding in your arms the child that you have just given birth to and say a prayer in your own words to the Guardian Angel Raziel. Stand in front of your altar, raise your hands high above your head and say these words:

Vesta, Vesta hear my plea,
Let my own child come to me,
Let my child of good health be.
Vesta, Vesta hear my plea.
And it harm none so be it.

Allow your candles to burn through to the end or put them out with a candle snuff. When you are finished working, move quietly to the left of your circle.

Extinguish the east candle and say:
   I thank the element of air for blessing me with fertility.

Extinguish the south candle and say:
   I thank the element of fire for blessing me with fertility.

Extinguish the west candle and say:
   I thank the element of water for blessing me with fertility.

Extinguish the north candle and say:
   I thank the element of earth for blessing me with fertility.

Close your circle by saying:
   May the four powers give back to the universe any powers
   and energies that have not been used.
   The work is now done and the circle is closed.
   So mote it be.

Fertility spell 2

10 mls almond oil
Frankincense pure essential oil
A bottle for your oil mixture
A small face cloth or some tissues
A small fireproof dish for matches or burning herbs or paper
A red tablecloth
Some pieces of moonstone
A sprig of birch
One white and one red taper candle and holders
One small pointed knife
A small dish to which you have added a pinch of dried basil

Prepare a blend of oils using 10 mls of almond oil and add three drops of frankincense pure essential oil. Hold the bottle of oil in your hands in the prayer position and rub the bottle vigorously between the palms of your hands and as you do so visualise the oil being empowered with gratitude. When you feel as though the oil has been charged place it on your altar or work surface ready for use along with the other items.

Place four small candles at the east, south, west and north in that order. Sit or kneel comfortably in front of your table. Close your eyes and as you breathe in, picture positive white light energy filling your body. When you are completely relaxed stand up and move quietly to the east quarter of your room.

Light the east candle and say:
May the element of air bless this space with light, love and air and make me fertile.

Light the south candle and say:
May the element of fire bless this space with light, love and fire and make me fertile.

Light the west candle and say:
May the element of water bless this space with light, love and water and make me fertile.

Light the north candle and say:
May the element of earth bless this space with light, love and earth and make me fertile.

Move quietly back to your workspace and kneel in front of your table. Light your white altar candle and meditate quietly on Goddess Vesta. Take your red spell candle and the small pointed knife and inscribe the numbers one and three and the rune symbols Beork and Wynn at the top of the candle. Place the candle back in the holder and taking the bottle of empowered oil place some in the palm of your hands. Rub your hands together and visualise that you are charging the energy in the oil and in your hands. Your hands will begin to feel very warm. Take the spell candle and spread the oil from middle to top and middle to bottom of the candle until the candle is completely covered in oil. Visualise that you are empowering the candle with fertility. Rub your hands vigorously together with the candle still held between the palms of your hands. After a few minutes, place your candle back in its holder and light the flame and say these words:

Ripe as seeds grow blessed with life
Fertile be my love, my life,
Sacred be this spell this day,
Fertility to come my way.
And it harm none so mote it be.

Allow your candle to burn for as long as possible but, if you must put it out, do not blow it out otherwise you will reverse or negate your spell. You can use a candle snuff or pinch the flame between your thumb and finger. You may light your candle again but each time you do so visualise your wish as though it has already begun to happen. When you are finished working, clean your hands on the cloth and move quietly to the left of your room.

Extinguish the east candle and say:
    I thank the element of air for blessing me with fertility.

Extinguish the south candle and say:
    I thank the element of fire for blessing me with fertility.

Extinguish the west candle and say:
    I thank the element of water for blessing me so that I may have happy home.

Extinguish the north candle and say:
    I thank the element of earth for blessing me so that I may have happy home.

Close your circle by saying:
    May the four powers give back to the universe any powers and energies that have not been used.
    The work is now done and the circle is closed.
    So mote it be.

20 Friendship

Day of the week: The best day of the week is Monday

Time of day: The best time of day is 5am. Also noon, 7pm or at any time in the evening when the moon is waxing or full but not when it is waning

Goddess: Luna

Planet: Moon

Guardian Angel: Gabriel

Star Sign: Cancer

Metal: Silver

Colour: White, silver, orange and yellow

Rune: Geofu (also known as Gefu), Eolh

Symbol: Pairs of things

Number: Any even number (2, 4, 6, 8 ...)

Crystal: Moonstone

Flower: Freesia

Essential oil: Patchouli

Tree: Silver birch

Herb: Fennel

Moon

Cancer

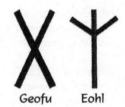

Geofu   Eohl

Friendship spell 1

Prepare yourself and decorate your work surface or altar space with all your chosen ingredients such as:

A cloth coloured white, silver orange or yellow
Some pieces of silver or silver friendship rings or tokens
Any suitable items that come in pairs
A piece of moonstone
A vase of freesia
A sprig of birch

When you are ready and everything is in place, stand at the edge of your circle. Close your eyes and breathe in, visualising light energy filling your body. Breathe out and breathe away all negative energy. When you are completely relaxed stand up and move quietly to the east quarter of your circle or room.

Light the east candle and say:
   May the element of air bless this space with light, love and air and grant me true friendship.

Light the south candle and say:
   May the element of fire bless this space with light, love and fire and grant me true friendship.

Light the west candle and say:
   May the element of water bless this space with light, love and water and grant me true friendship.

Light the north candle and say:
   May the element of earth bless this space with light, love and earth and grant me true friendship.

Move quietly back to your workspace and kneel in front of your table. Light your white altar candle and meditate quietly on the Goddess Luna. In your mind see yourself among true friends, laughing, happy and content, well liked by all who know you.

Say a prayer in your own words to your Guardian Angel and, standing in front of your altar, raise your hands high above your head and say these words:

Friends may come and friends may go
But true friends stay forever.
Merry we meet and merry we part,
Happy when we're together.
And it harm none so mote it be.

Spend some quiet time in your circle and allow your candles to burn through to the end or put them out with a candle snuff. When you are finished working move quietly to the left of your circle.

Extinguish the east candle and say:
I thank the element of air for blessing me with loyal, loving friends.

Extinguish the south candle and say:
I thank the element of fire for blessing me with loyal, loving friends.

Extinguish the west candle and say:
I thank the element of water for blessing me with loyal, loving friends.

Extinguish the north candle and say:
I thank the element of earth for blessing me with loyal, loving friends.

Close your circle by saying:
May the four powers give back to the universe any powers and energies that have not been used.
The work is now done and the circle is closed.
So mote it be.

Friendship spell 2

10 mls almond oil
Patchouli pure essential oil
A bottle for your oil mixture
A white tablecloth
A small face cloth or some tissues
A small fireproof dish for matches or burning herbs or paper
One white and one pink taper candle and holders
One small pointed knife
A sprig of silver birch
A small dish of dried fennel
A piece of moonstone

Prepare a blend of oils using 10 mls of almond oil and add three drops of patchouli pure essential oil. Hold the bottle of oil in your hands in the prayer position and rub the bottle vigorously between the palms of your hands and as you do so visualise the oil being empowered with friendship. When you feel as though the oil has been charged place it on your altar or work surface ready for use along with the other items.

Place four small candles at the east, south, west and north in that order. Sit or kneel comfortably in front of your table. Close your eyes and as you breathe in, picture positive white light energy filling your body. When you are completely relaxed stand up and move quietly to the east quarter of your room.

Light the east candle and say:
> May the element of air bless this space with light, love and air, and loyal friends.

Light the south candle and say:
> May the element of fire bless this space with light, love and fire, and loyal friends.

Light the west candle and say:
> May the element of water bless this space with light, love and water, and loyal friends.

Light the north candle and say:
> May the element of earth bless this space with light, love and earth, and loyal friends.

Move quietly back to your workspace and kneel in front of your table. Light your white altar candle and meditate quietly on the Goddess Luna. Take your pink spell candle and the small pointed knife and inscribe even numbers and the rune symbols Geofu and Eolh at the top of the candle. Place the candle back in the holder and taking the bottle of empowered oil place some in the palms of your hands. Rub your hands together and visualise that you are charging the energy in the oil and in your hands. Your hands will begin to feel very warm. Take the spell candle and spread the oil from middle to top and middle to bottom of the candle until the candle is completely covered in oil. Visualise that you are empowering your candle with friendship. Rub your hands vigorously together with the candle still held between the palms of your hands.

After a few minutes, place your candle back in its holder and light the flame and say these words:

> Luna, Goddess of the moon,
> Let my friends come to me soon.
> May they be loyal and be kind,
> And may they be of like mind.
> And it harm none so mote it be.

Allow your altar candle to burn through to the end or put it out with a candle snuff. You may light your candle again but each time you do so visualise your wish as though it has already begun to happen. When you are finished working clean your hands on the cloth and move quietly to the left of your room.

Extinguish the east candle and say:
> I thank the element of air for blessing me with loyal and loving friends.

Extinguish the south candle and say:
> I thank the element of fire for blessing me with loyal and loving friends.

Extinguish the west candle and say:
> I thank the element of water for blessing me with loyal and loving friends.

Extinguish the north candle and say:
> I thank the element of earth for blessing me with loyal and loving friends.

Close your circle by saying:
> May the four powers give back to the universe any powers and energies that have not been used.
> The work is now done and the circle is closed.
> So mote it be.

21 Passion

Day of the week: The best day of the week is Tuesday

Time of Day: The best time of day is 5am. Also noon, 7pm or at any time in the evening when the moon is waxing or full but not when it is waning

Goddess: Lillith

Planet: Venus

Guardian Angel: Gamelie

Star Sign: Scorpio, Taurus and Libra

Metal: Copper and brass

Colour: Red, orange and green

Rune: Ing (also known as Ingux)

Symbol: Fire

Number: One

Crystal: Emerald and sapphire

Flower: Poppy and tiger lily

Essential oil: Patchouli

Tree: Pine

Herb: Fennel

Venus

Scorpio   Taurus

Libra

Ing

Passion spell 1

Prepare yourself and decorate your work surface or altar space with all your chosen ingredients such as:

A red cloth
A piece of emerald, sapphire or ruby jewellery
Small items made of copper or brass
One white and one red taper candle and holders
A vase of poppies or tiger lilies
A sprig of pine

When you are ready and everything is in place, stand at the edge of your circle. Close your eyes and breathe in, visualising light energy filling your body. Breathe out and breathe away all negative energy. When you are completely relaxed stand up and move quietly to the east quarter of your circle or room.

Light the east candle and say:
    May the element of air bless this space with light, love and
    air and bring passion into my life.

Light the south candle and say:
    May the element of fire bless this space with light, love and
    fire and bring passion into my life.

Light the west candle and say:
    May the element of water bless this space with light, love
    and water and bring passion into my life.

Light the north candle and say:
    May the element of earth bless this space with light, love
    and earth and bring passion into my life.

Move quietly back to your workspace and kneel in front of your table. Light your white altar candle and meditate quietly on the Goddess Lilith.
    Say a prayer in your own words to the Guardian Angel Gamelie and, standing in front of your altar, raise your hands high above your head and say these words:

                    Passion burns within my loins –
                        My heart, my soul, a-fire.
                    Lillith bring to me this night
                        The passion I desire.
                    And it harm none so be it.

Spend some quiet time in your circle and allow your altar candles to burn through to the end or put them out with a candle snuff. When you are finished working, move quietly to the left of your circle.

Extinguish the east candle and say:
   I thank the element of air for blessing me with passion.

Extinguish the south candle and say:
   I thank the element of fire for blessing me with passion.

Extinguish the west candle and say:
   I thank the element of water for blessing me with passion.

Extinguish the north candle and say:
   I thank the element of earth for blessing me with passion.

Close your circle by saying:
   *May the four powers give back to the universe any powers
   and energies that have not been used.
   The work is now done and the circle is closed.
   So mote it be.*

Passion spell 2

10 mls almond oil
Patchouli pure essential oil
A bottle for your oil mixture
A red tablecloth
A small face cloth or some tissues
A small fireproof dish for matches or burning herbs or paper
One white and one red taper candle and holders
One small pointed knife
A deep red crystal or some ruby emerald or sapphire jewellery
A vase of poppies
A small dish containing some hazelnuts

Prepare a blend of oils using 10 mls of almond oil and add three drops of patchouli pure essential oil. Hold the bottle of oil in your hands in the prayer position and rub the bottle vigorously between the palms of your hands and as you do so visualise the oil being empowered with passion. When you feel as though the oil has been charged, place it on your altar or work surface ready for use along with the other items.

Place four small candles at the east, south, west and north in that order. Sit or kneel comfortably in front of your table. Close your eyes and as you breathe in, picture positive white light energy filling your body. When you are completely relaxed stand up and move quietly to the east quarter of your room.

Light the east candle and say:
   May the element of air bless this space with light, love and air and bring passion into my life.

Light the south candle and say:
   May the element of fire bless this space with light, love and fire and bring passion into my life.

Light the west candle and say:
   May the element of water bless this space with light, love and water and bring passion into my life.

Light the north candle and say:
   May the element of earth bless this space with light, love and earth and bring passion into my life.

Move quietly back to your workspace and kneel in front of your table. Light your white altar candle and meditate quietly on the Goddess Lillith. Take your red spell candle and the small pointed knife and inscribe the number one and the rune symbol Ing at the top of the candle. Place the candle back in the holder and, taking the bottle of empowered oil, place some in the palms of your hands. Rub your hands together and visualise that you are charging the energy in the oil and in your hands. Your hands will begin to feel very warm.

Take the spell candle and spread the oil from middle to top and middle to bottom of the candle until the candle is completely covered in oil. Visualise that you are empowering your candle with passion. Rub your hands vigorously together with the candle still held between the palms of your hands. After a few minutes, place your candle back in its holder and light the flame and say these words:

> *Strong in me doth passion burn*
> *Bliss is what my soul doth yearn*
> *Candle take this wish of mine*
> *Blessed above, from the Divine.*
> *And it harm none so mote it be.*

Allow your altar candle to burn through to the end or put it out with a candle snuff. You may light your candle again but each time you do so visualise your wish as though it has already begun to happen. When you are finished working clean your hands on the cloth and move quietly to the left of your room.

Extinguish the east candle and say:
I thank the element of air for blessing me with passion.

Extinguish the south candle and say:
I thank the element of fire for blessing me with passion.

Extinguish the west candle and say:
I thank the element of water for blessing me with passion.

Extinguish the north candle and say:
I thank the element of earth for blessing me with passion.

Close your circle by saying:
*May the four powers give back to the universe any powers
and energies that have not been used.
The work is now done and the circle is closed.
So mote it be.*

22 Answers

Day of the week: The best day of the week is Wednesday
Time of day: The best time of day is 5am. Also noon, 7pm or at any time in the evening when the moon is waxing or full but not when it is waning
Goddess: Themis
Planet: Mercury
Star sign: Gemini or Virgo
Metal: Quicksilver
Colour: Orange, yellow or green
Rune: Ansur (also known as Ansuz)
Symbol: Books or calculators
Number: Nine
Crystal: Opal, aquamarine, hematite or jet
Flower: Lavender
Herb: Angelica
Essential oil: Marjoram
Tree: Oak

Mercury

Gemini   Virgo

Ansur

Answers spell 1

Prepare yourself and decorate your work surface or altar space with all your chosen ingredients such as:

A yellow or green cloth
A vase of lavender
A dictionary
A thesaurus
A calculator
A piece of opal or aquamarine
One yellow and one white taper candle and holders

When you are ready and everything is in place, stand at the edge of your circle. Close your eyes and breathe in, visualising light energy filling your body. Breathe out and breathe away all negative energy. When you are completely relaxed, stand up and move quietly to the east quarter of your circle or room.

Light the east candle and say:
> May the element of air bless this space with light, love and air and help me find the answers to my question.

Light the south candle and say:
> May the element of fire bless this space with light, love and fire and help me find the answers to my question.

Light the west candle and say:
> May the element of water bless this space with light, love and water and help me find the answers to my question.

Light the north candle and say:
> May the element of earth bless this space with light, love and earth and help me find the answers to my question.

Move quietly back to your workspace and kneel in front of your table. Light your white altar candle and meditate quietly on the Goddess Themis. In your mind see your answers coming to you. Say a prayer in your own words to your Guardian Angel and ask for guidance.

Stand in front of your altar, raise your hands high above your head and say these words:

Answers come to me in sleep
So they can be mine to keep.
They give me guidance, clear and true
So that I may know what's sure.
And it harm none so be it.

Spend some quiet time in your circle and allow your altar candles to
burn through to the end or put them out with a candle snuff. When
you are finished working move quietly to the left of your circle.

Extinguish the east candle and say:
I thank the element of air for blessing me with the answers
that make things clear.

Extinguish the south candle and say:
I thank the element of fire for blessing me with the answers
that make things clear.

Extinguish the west candle and say:
I thank the element of water for blessing me with the
answers that make things clear.

Extinguish the north candle and say:
I thank the element of earth for blessing me with the answers
that make things clear.

Close your circle by saying:
May the four powers give back to the universe any powers
and energies that have not been used.
The work is now done and the circle is closed.
So mote it be.

Answers spell 2

10mls almond oil
Marjoram pure essential oil
A bottle for your oil mixture
A orange yellow or green tablecloth
A small face cloth or some tissues and a small fireproof dish for
matches or burning herbs or paper.
One white and one green taper candle and holders
One small pointed knife
A piece of hematite or jet
A sprig of oak
A small dish containing some angelica

Prepare a blend of oils using 10 mls of almond oil and add three drops of marjoram pure essential oil. Hold the bottle of oil in your hands in the prayer position and rub the bottle vigorously between the palms of your hands and as you do so visualise the oil being empowered with the answers to your questions. When you feel as though the oil has been charged place it on your altar or work surface ready for use along with the other items.

Place four small candles at the east, south, west and north in that order. Sit or kneel comfortably in front of your table. Close your eyes and as you breathe in, picture positive white light energy filling your body. When you are completely relaxed stand up and move quietly to the east quarter of your room.

Light the east candle and say:
  May the element of air bless this space with light, love and air and help me find the answers to my question.

Light the south candle and say:
  May the element of fire bless this space with light, love and fire and help me find the answers to my question.

Light the west candle and say:
  May the element of water bless this space with light, love and Water and help me find the answers to my question.

Light the north candle and say:
  May the element of earth bless this space with light, love and earth and help me find the answers to my question.

Move quietly back to your workspace and kneel in front of your table. Light your white altar candle and meditate quietly on the problem that perplexes you. Take your green spell candle and the small pointed knife and inscribe the number nine and the rune symbol Ansur at the top of the candle. Place the candle back in the holder and, taking the bottle of empowered oil, place some in the palm of your hands. Rub your hands together and visualise that you are charging the energy in the oil and in your hands. Your hands will begin to feel very warm. Take the spell candle and spread the oil from middle to top and middle to bottom of the candle until the candle is completely covered in oil. Visualise that you are empowering your candle with the answers that you are looking for. Rub your hands vigorously together with the candle still held between the palms of your hands.

After a few minutes, place your candle back in its holder and light the flame and say these words:

> Answers, may they come to me
> So that I may clearly see
> What is hidden from me now
> Will be shown to me somehow.
> And it harm none so mote it be.

Allow your altar candle to burn through to the end or put it out with a candle snuff. You may light your candle again but, each time you do so, visualise your wish as though it has already begun to happen. When you are finished working, clean your hands on the cloth and move quietly to the left of your room.

Extinguish the east candle and say:
> I thank the element of air for granting me the answers I require.

Extinguish the south candle and say:
> I thank the element of fire for granting me the answers I require.

Extinguish the west candle and say:
> I thank the element of water for granting me the answers I require.

Extinguish the north candle and say:
> I thank the element of earth for granting me the answers I require.

Close your circle by saying:
> May the four powers give back to the universe any powers and energies that have not been used.
> The work is now done and the circle is closed.
> So mote it be.

23 Travel

Day of the week: The best day of the week is Tuesday
Time of day: The best time of day is 5am. Also noon, 7pm or at any time in the evening when the moon is waxing or full but not when it is waning
Goddess: Dag
Planet: Uranus
Guardian Angel: Michael
Star sign: Sagittarius
Metal: Radium
Colour: Pale blue
Rune: Rad
Symbol: Passports, tickets, maps, wheels or spheres
Number: 19
Crystal: Turquoise or chrysolite
Flower: Yellow daisy
Essential oil: Basil
Herb: Caraway
Tree: Oak

Uranus

Sagittarius

Rad

Travel spell 1

Prepare yourself and decorate your work surface or altar space with all your chosen ingredients such as:

A blue cloth and a vase of yellow daisies
A piece of chrysolite
One blue and one white taper candle and holders
A sprig of oak
Some maps, a passport or tickets

When you are ready and everything is in place, stand at the edge of your circle. Close your eyes and breathe in, visualising light energy filling your body. Breathe out and breathe away all negative energy. When you are completely relaxed stand up and move quietly to the east quarter of your circle or room.

Light the east candle and say:
    May the element of air bless this space with light, love and air and fulfil my desire to travel in safety to …

Light the south candle and say:
    May the element of fire bless this space with light, love and fire and fulfil my desire to travel in safety to …

Light the west candle and say:
    May the element of water bless this space with light, love and water and fulfil my desire to travel in safety to …

Light the north candle and say:
    May the element of earth bless this space with light, love and earth and fulfil my desire to travel in safety to …

Move quietly back to your workspace and kneel in front of your table. Light your white altar candle and meditate quietly on the Goddess Dag. In your mind see your journey being planned, undertaken and visualise that you are arriving at your destination safely. Say a prayer in your own words to the Guardian Angel Michael.

Stand in front of your altar, raise your hands high above your head and say these words:

A journey to (place) I plan to make
Precious things with me I take
Safe and sure my trip will be
Dag I thank you, blessed be
And it harm none so be it.

Spend some quiet time in your circle and allow your altar candles to burn through to the end or put them out with a candle snuff. When you are finished working move quietly to the left of your circle.

Extinguish the east candle and say:
    I thank the element of air for blessing me with a safe journey.

Extinguish the south candle and say:
    I thank the element of fire for blessing me with a safe journey.

Extinguish the west candle and say:
    I thank the element of water for blessing me with a safe journey.

Extinguish the north candle and say:
    I thank the element of earth for blessing me with a safe journey.

Close your circle by saying:
    May the four powers give back to the universe any powers and energies that have not been used.
    The work is now done and the circle is closed.
    So mote it be.

Travel spell 2

10 mls almond oil
Basil pure essential oil
A bottle or your oil mixture
A pale blue tablecloth
Passports, tickets, maps, wheels or spheres
A small face cloth or some tissues
A small fireproof dish for matches or burning herbs or paper.
One white and one pale blue taper candle and holders
One small pointed knife
A piece of turquoise or chrysolite
A vase or posy of yellow daisies
A small dish containing some dried caraway

Prepare a blend of oils using 10 mls of almond oil and add three drops of basil pure essential oil. Hold the bottle of oil in your hands in the prayer position and rub the bottle vigorously between the palms of your hands and as you do so visualise the oil being empowered with safe travel. When you feel as though the oil has been charged, place it on your altar or work surface ready for use along with the other items.

Place four small candles at the east, south, west and north in that order. Sit or kneel comfortably in front of your table. Close your eyes and as you breathe in, picture positive white light energy filling your body. When you are completely relaxed, stand up and move quietly to the east quarter of your room.

Light the east candle and say:

May the element of air bless this space with light, love and air and fulfil my desire to travel in safety to …

Light the south candle and say:

May the element of fire bless this space with light, love and fire and fulfil my desire to travel in safety to …

Light the west candle and say:

May the element of water bless this space with light, love and water and fulfil my desire to travel in safety to …

Light the north candle and say:

May the element of earth bless this space with light, love and earth and fulfil my desire to travel in safety to …

Move quietly back to your workspace and kneel in front of your table. Light your white altar candle and meditate quietly on the Goddess Dag. Take your pale blue spell candle and the small pointed knife and inscribe the number 19 and the rune symbol Rad at the top of the candle.

Place the candle back in the holder and taking the bottle of empowered oil place some in the palm, of your hands. Rub your hands together and visualise that you are charging the energy in the oil and in your hands. Your hands will begin to feel very warm.

Take the spell candle and spread the oil from middle to top and middle to bottom of the candle until the candle is completely covered in oil. Visualise that you are empowering your candle with a safe journey. Rub your hands vigorously together with the candle still held between the palms of your hands.

After a few minutes, place your candle back in its holder and light the flame and say these words:

Keep me safe and free from harm
On this journey I do plan.
Day or night I will get there,
Dag, my plan with you I share.
And it harm none so be it.

Allow your altar candle to burn through to the end or put it out with a candle snuff. You may light your candle again but each time you do so visualise your wish as though it has already begun to happen. When you are finished working, clean your hands on the cloth and move quietly to the left of your room.

Extinguish the east candle and say:
I thank the element of air for blessing me with a safe journey.

Extinguish the south candle and say:
I thank the element of fire for blessing me with a safe journey.

Extinguish the west candle and say:
I thank the element of water for blessing me with a safe journey.

Extinguish the north candle and say:
I thank the element of earth for blessing me with a safe journey.

Close your circle by saying:
May the four powers give back to the universe any powers and energies that have not been used.
The work is now done and the circle is closed.
So mote it be.

Runes

The runes are an ancient Nordic form of script used before the emergence of written language, taking the form of straight lines which were easily cut into wood or stone. It is not known exactly how old they are but they may originate as early as the Bronze Age.

'Runa' means 'mystery' or 'secret proceedings' and runes are a marvellous aid to magic because the symbols are easy to draw or inscribe and each rune has its own significance.

Feoh

Sometimes called: Fehu
Meaning: Cattle
Its significance in magik: For wealth, property, power and status.

Ur

Sometimes called: Uruz
Meaning: Aurochs, ox-like
    beasts
Its significance in magik:
    Overcoming challenges,
    passing tests and anything
    that requires effort on your
    part.

Thorn

Sometimes called: Thurizas
Meaning: Thorn
Its significance in magik: Could
    be used to help rid yourself
    of a problem.

Ansur

Sometimes called: Ansuz
Meaning: A god
Its significance in magik: For
communication.

Rad

Sometimes called: Rado and
Raidho
Meaning: Riding
Its significance in magik: For
travel plans or anything
that is connected with
movement.

Ken

Sometimes called: Kano, or
    Kenaz
Meaning: Torch
Its significance in magik: For
    openings and invitations.

Geofu

Sometimes called: Gefu and
    Gebo
Meaning: Gift
Its significance in magik: For
    partnerships and unions,
    marriages or engagements.

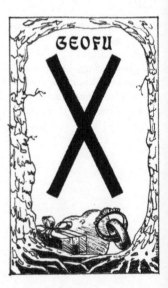

Wynn

Sometimes called: Wunjo
Meaning: Joy
Its significance in magik: For joy,
   success and winning.

Hagall

Sometimes called: The Aett or
   Set of Hagalaz or Heimdall,
   Watcher of the Gods
Meaning: Hail
Its significance in magik: For
   projects or situations that
   demand sudden, unex-
   pected changes.

Nied

Sometimes called: Naudhiz or
    Nauthiz
Meaning: Need
Its significance in magik: To
    place restrictions on prob-
    lem areas.

Is

Sometimes called: Isa
Meaning: Ice
Its significance in magik: For
    where caution is required
    and where you may be
    tempted to act in haste.

Yr

Sometimes known as : Eiwaz
Meaning: Yew
Its significance in magik: For
  projects that demand con-
  tinuous effort.

Peorth

Sometimes called: Perth or
  Perthro
Meaning: Lot-cup
Its significance in magik:
  For secrets and hidden
  information.

Eolh

Sometimes called: Elhaz or
  Algiz
Meaning: Elk-Sedge
Its significance in magik: For
  friendship and protection.

Sigel

Sometimes called: Sowilo
Meaning: Sun
Its significance in magik: For
  victory.

Tir

Sometimes called: The Aett of
    Tiwaz, Tiwaz
Meaning: Star
Its significance in magik: For
    winning where competition
    is fierce.

Beork

Sometimes called: Berkano or
    Berkana
Meaning: Birch
Its significance in magik: For
    rebirth, new beginnings and
    fertility.

Eoh

Sometimes called: Ehwaz
Meaning: Horse
Its significance in magik: For
   stability and property.

Mann

Sometimes called: Manaz
Meaning: Man
Its significance in magik: For
   a helping hand or a true,
   sharing friendship.

Lagu

Sometimes called: Laguz
Meaning: Water
Its significance in magik: For
    water-related topics and the
    feminine element.

Ing

Sometimes called Inguz or
    Ingwaz
Meaning: The God Ing, God of
    the Hearth and the counter-
    part of Nerthus the Earth
    Mother
Its significance in magik: For
    fertility and bliss.

Daeg

Sometimes called: Dagaz
Meaning: Day
Its significance in magik: For
    hope and promise.

Othel

Sometimes called: Othillo or
    Othala
Meaning: Homestead
Its significance in magik:
    For the home, family and
    integrity.

Jara

Sometimes called: Gera
Meaning: Harvest
Its significance in magik: You
will reap what you sow.
Efforts made will be justly
rewarded. The more effort
put in, the greater the
reward.

Wyrd

More difficult to represent on
a candle is the Wyrd rune
because it is blank and it
stands for the inevitable. To
use this rune it is important
to be really focused, and
to illustrate it, simply draw
a square with the corners
rounded off and visualise
the inevitable.

Numerology

Some people will say that they are typical of their astrological star sign whilst others will say that they are nothing like theirs. Why is that so? Did you know that the numbers in your date of birth play a very large part in forming your character? In fact these numbers will motivate and mould you, and their influence will be with you for the rest of your life.

Numbers are important because they have their own significance and power. Numerologists believe that the numbers one to nine have specific characteristics.

Numerology is the name given to the ancient method of studying numbers that has been in use for thousands of years. It gives insight into people's personalities and their motivation in life. It is an ancient practice that is used to analyse people's characters.

The most popular form of numerology in use today is based on the work of Pythagoras, the famous Greek mathematician and philosopher who lived during the sixth century bc.

Pythagoras believed that numbers were the first of all things in nature. It was his belief that numbers were the basis of everything, in the natural, spiritual and scientific world. He believed that everything could be reduced to mathematical terms and that everything had a numerical value. Pythagoras, who believed that numbers created order and beauty, founded a school for students to follow his philosophy, and this was known as the Italic or Pythagorean school.

As an avid numerologist I was amazed to discover recently that the age difference between myself and my husband Martin is seven years, seven months and seven days. Seven, which is a mystical number, is also my lucky number. In fact, the numbers in my name also add up to seven.

To find your birth number

Your birthday holds the key to the most significant number in your life. To find it, you first need to write out your full date of birth in its numerical form.
For example:
21/04/1972
Add together the numbers in each section of your birth date:
$2 + 1 + 0 + 4 + 1 + 9 + 7 + 2 = 26$

Add these two numbers together to reduce the number to a single numeral within the range one to nine:
2 + 6 = 8
The birth number for this person is eight.

To find your name number

Name numbers are not tied to you in the way that birth numbers are. It is possible to change your name number. It is not possible to change your birth number.

Your name is a personal symbol. It has been chosen for you and you will react to it in your own individual way. The name that you choose to work with for the purposes of numerology is entirely up to you. It might include your middle name and your last name, or like me, you might just be known to most people by your first name.

The letters of the alphabet correspond to the numbers one to nine in the following way:

1	2	3	4	5	6	7	8	9
a	b	c	d	e	f	g	h	i
j	k	l	m	n	o	p	q	r
s	t	u	v	w	x	y	z	

So the name number for 'Soraya' would be calculated in the following way:

s   o   r   a   y   a
1 + 6 + 9 + 1 + 7 + 1 = 25
2 + 5 = 7
My name number is seven.

Key words, which describe the numerical influences

One
Leadership, popularity, decisiveness, construction.

Two
Diplomacy, tactfulness, secrets, unions and partnerships.

Three
Caring, compassionate, tender, friends and celebration.

Four

Dependable, ambitious, property, stability and security.

Five

Keys, opportunities, religion, engineering and answers.

Six

Relationships, choices, loving, loyal.

Seven

Wisdom, control, transport,

Eight

Stubbornness, strength, persistence.

Nine

Completion, results, reunions, pregnancy.

Using Herbs and Essential Oils

If you plan to work with herbs for healing purposes begin to prepare them on the new moon. Always use pure essential oils and not blends unless you have blended them yourself. Here are some helpful definitions, instructions and recipes.

Infusions

This process draws the properties you want out of the herb for healing. An infusion is rather like a strong tea. The normal mixture is 1 pint of water to half an ounce of herb. It takes experience to learn how long each herb needs to steep, some take longer than others. The average length of time is half an hour but with practice you'll learn which take longer and which take less time.

Decoctions

This is much the same as an infusion except you are working with thick pieces of root or bark, which can't be ground up.

When you are working with several herbs, begin with the toughest then work down. Start with cold water and, making sure that no steam escapes or the vital oils will be lost, boil for 30 minutes to an hour then allow the blend to steep for the same time.

Poultice

Pour boiling water over the herbs using just enough to dampen them or evenly cover the plants. When they are all evenly wet, remove them with a strainer and place between two pieces of fine cotton. Apply the poultice with the herbs inside to the affected area.

Ointments and salves

Heat some petroleum jelly or vegetable fat until it is quite warm and add the ground herbs to it. Strain and put into jars.

Washes

Theses should be made in the same way as teas and when they are ready they can be applied externally.

Tinctures

These are used when long-term storage is required and vodka is perfect although I use brandy and malt whisky for chest infections and coughs.

1–4 ounces of the herb
8 ounces of vodka, brandy or whisky
4 ounces of water

Seal the jar and keep it safely out of the light for two weeks. Every day for the two weeks shake the jar lightly to blend the ingredients. At the end of the two-week period, strain the blend and store in a dark jar in the refrigerator.

There are many minor ailments that can be eased by the use of herbs and plants that grow in the garden but the first thing to do is to buy or borrow from your local library some reference books which show plant illustrations as well as text. There is nothing worse than not being able to identify a plant that you want to use as a spell or remedy. Some plants can be very dangerous.

Marigold syrup

Marigold is one of my favourites, however, it must be the old fashioned *Calendula officinalis* and not the African or any other variety. It is antiseptic, anti-fungal, antidepressant, anti-inflammatory and it also strengthens the immune system. For women, calendula is especially helpful during the menstrual cycle or the menopause and, as if that was not enough, it can be made into a cream and applied to cuts and grazes to aid the healing process. Aemilius Macer in the 13th century, said that gazing at the flowers strengthened the eyesight:

> *'The golden flower is good to be seen, it*
> *makes the sight bright and clean.'*

My granddaughter Ashi calls the syrup I make from it 'Granny's Magik Syrup' and I use marigold petals in soups, salads and rice dishes as well as keeping a jar of the syrup in the fridge for any visitors who come and complain of a sore throat or a cold.

To make marigold syrup:

Marigold petals, enough to fill a two-pint pan
Boiling water
Brown or white sugar
Pure essential oil of calendula or pure essential oil of lavender

Fill a two-pint pan with marigold petals and add boiling water to reach almost to the top of the pan. Reduce the heat and allow the mixture to simmer until the volume has reduced by about two inches. Remove from the heat and allow to cool. When the mixture has cooled, strain the liquid through muslin cloth until the juices are extracted.

Using a cup or mug, measure the remaining marigold liquid. Put the liquid back into the pan and for each cup of liquid add the equivalent amount of brown or white sugar. Bring to the boil and as before, reduce the heat and allow to simmer until the mixture has reduced by about two inches. Remove the mixture from the heat and add two drops of pure essential oil of calendula. I have used lavender before and it is also really lovely. When the mixture is cool enough put into sterilised jars and store in the fridge.

For depression

A teaspoonful of marigold syrup when you are feeling down will lift your spirits but, if you really have the blues, take it three to four times a day or make a tea with the petals.

Sore throat remedy

If you have a sore throat take one teaspoonful three times a day. Hold it in your mouth for a moment and let it slowly trickle down your throat.

Fever

Safe for children, marigold petals can be used as a tea to help to reduce fever especially if the neck glands are swollen.

Do not assume that this replaces medical treatment. It does not.

Dry cough mix

4 tablespoons of honey,
4 drops of pure essential oil of eucalyptus,
4 drops of pure essential oil of lemon
Brandy or whisky

Put the honey, essential oil of eucalyptus, essential oil of lemon and a good measure of brandy or whisky into a clean, dark coloured medicine bottle. Shake the mixture thoroughly until all the ingredients are well mixed. One teaspoonful of this mixture can be diluted in a small glass of warm water and taken as and when it is required. Remember that this remedy contains alcohol, and therefore you cannot drink a lot of this and drive, no matter how good it tastes!

Useful Contacts

For dried petals, herbs, essential oils, creams, blends, lotions, incenses, charcoals, crystals and candles:
    Soraya
    Email: info@soraya.co.uk
    Web: www.soraya.co.uk

For membership of the Pagan Federation or the quarterly magazine *Pagan Dawn*:
    The Pagan Federation
    BM Box 7079
    London
    WC1N 3XX

For Christenings (Naming Ceremonies) Handfastings or Bereavements:
    The Life Rites Group
    Gwndwn Mawr
    Trelech
    Carmarthenshire
    SA33 6SA
    Tel: 01994 484527
    Email: Info@LifeRites.org